Outdoor Education

Outdoor Education
*by T M Parker
and K I Meldrum*

J M Dent and Sons Limited London

Made in Great Britain at the
Aldine Press · Letchworth · Herts
for J M Dent & Sons Limited
26 Albemarle Street · London W1X 4QY

Boards ISBN 0 460 09585 4
Limp ISBN 0 460 09617 6

Contents

Acknowledgments

We have been able to write this book largely as a result of our accumulated knowledge gained through personal experience and involvement in the teaching, organizing and administration of outdoor education over a number of years. Through this experience we are conscious of our debt to all the other workers in this field; the historical section of the book clearly indicates over what a long period this debt has accrued. Although everyone we approached has willingly co-operated and has encouraged us in this enterprise we feel that we should record our particular gratitude to the following people and organizations who have so generously given of their time, opinions and advice and who have permitted our use of unpublished materials:

L. Hunter	Moray House College of Education
K. Pearce	Boreatton Park School, Shropshire
H. Brown	Braehead School, Fife
G. Slee	Northumberland Education Committee
K. Oldham	Whitehough Camp School, Lancashire
R. Davies	George Pindar School, Scarborough
T. Churchill	Wolverhampton Education Committee
I. Mackay	Edinburgh Schools Sailing Association
W. Keay	Bingley College of Education
D. Roscoe	Loughborough College of Education
D. Dean	Abbotsholme School, Derbyshire

R. Blain   National Trust for Scotland
D. Pashley   Napier College, Edinburgh
                Edinburgh Education Committee
                Derbyshire Education Committee

We hope that all those who have helped will feel that their contributions have been of value.

Introduction

So much is being written and said about conservation, population and recreation that it is inevitable for education and its role in affecting these issues to become an aspect of some importance. Of course, there are many sections of education which have a significant part to play, but the concern of this book is with outdoor education and especially with the potential and the problems of using the countryside as a means of education.

'Some outdoor experiences are inspirational, or educational, or simply enjoyable. Others are mediocre and still others inferior, some to the point of negative value or dissatisfaction.' This statement in Clawson and Knetsch's book *The Economics of Outdoor Recreation* faces us with the probability that there is nothing intrinsically more valuable in teaching in the outdoors than teaching in the classroom. Throughout the book this probability is borne in mind and we have concentrated on outlining and examining the ways in which outdoor education should be provided for, organized, conducted and developed in order that it might be as effective a teaching method as many people claim.

One of our first tasks is to define the role and function of outdoor education. The following titles are frequently used loosely as synonyms for outdoor education and clearly illustrate the dichotomy which for too long has polarized the elements of physical activity and academic studies.

Outdoor Living   Environmental Education
Outdoor Action   Environmental Studies

Outdoor Studies	Environmental Science
Outdoor Pursuits	Rural Studies
Outdoor Activities	Rural and Environmental Studies
Outdoor Sports	Ecology and Conservation
Outdoor Recreation	Field Studies
Open Country Pursuits	Nature Studies
Adventure Activity	Natural Sciences
Outward Bound	Conservation Education
	Countryside Studies

It is appropriate to quote the following extract from a report by the Council for Environmental Education: 'The term environmental education is being used increasingly in Britain but it is clear that different people mean different things by it and also that some who use it are not really certain what they mean.'

Although we go on to look in greater detail at what we mean by outdoor education we accept the definition of it originated by the National Association for Outdoor Education: 'Outdoor Education is a means of approaching educational objectives through guided direct experience in the environment, using its resources as learning materials,' and see it as a combination of the techniques of outdoor pursuits and countryside studies leading to a wide range of educational experiences. Although we are concerned in the book with outdoor education's role in providing opportunities for young people to try pursuits which may be retained for adult leisure time, and its contribution towards educating people into proper use of the countryside, we recognize that it has considerably more than just those two aspects to offer and in chapter one we attempt to describe and give examples of all the facets of outdoor education.

The pattern of the book emerges in the first chapter. We feel that it is entirely relevant to refer constantly to national issues, attitudes and practices and relate educational developments to these so that they can be kept in perspective. Chapter two traces through the same pattern the historical growth of pursuits and studies using the environment as the common factor and chapter three looks critically at present-day facilities, provisions and methods especially in education authorities, schools and centres. Chapter four goes on to outline both the existing and the essential training and qualification schemes available to students and teachers.

There is no doubt in our minds that outdoor education, if it is to continue to be encouraged by government policies and local support, should be based on progressive programmes in schools. It is our contention that at the moment a great deal too much is left to chance or voluntary efforts rather than to design or a structured system. Until there is a large number of fully trained teachers available then the schools cannot be expected to implement a continuous related programme of outdoor education for all pupils.

In order that we could provide what we hope are logical, practical suggestions for the future we chose to refer to policies and practices in other countries mainly in Europe and North America in chapter five and then gather together our own experiences and beliefs and what we have learned from others in the last chapter. There is the undoubted necessity to consider critically the work that is going on in outdoor education in universities, colleges, schools and centres and attempt to produce from a variety of differing philosophies, methods and practices an educationally sound core of knowledge and to achieve an acceptable structure in order that knowledge, quality, inspiration, individual potential and responsibility, all ingredients of true education, provide the reasoning behind introducing young people to activity and study in the countryside.

It is hoped that this book, with its fundamental approach through national patterns and development related to educational practices and philosophies, will be of value to those responsible for determining educational policies in outdoor education. Its practical approach should assist teachers to make fuller use of the time available in a school curriculum. As the only book outlining the historical development of outdoor education and detailing current practices it will provide an essential text book for students who intend to work in this field. The bibliographies included with each chapter together with the appendices form a useful reference for further reading in a wide range of aspects.

Lastly, we hope that the book will make it possible for a new generation to take advantage of the countryside through a structured programme which by progressive exposure will provide a lasting source of pleasure and will stimulate an intelligent response to the manifold problems which increasing use and awareness of the countryside will demand.

Chapter One

The roles, aims and objectives of outdoor education

Many of the well-established subjects on a school, college or university curriculum list have had to undergo periods of introspection and produce sophisticated justification for their existence. Outdoor education is no exception. In order to attempt to clarify the present educational situation it is necessary to grapple with the multiplicity of approaches to the use of the environment and to detail the most important factors which are emerging, but first of all it is essential to outline the relevant background which it might be conjectured has provided stimulation to the expansion of work in schools.

RELEVANT ISSUES OF CONSERVATION AND LEISURE

It is likely that the population of Britain will double in the lifetime of a child born in 1970, and as the number of people affects everything fundamentally then this fact is most relevant. The obvious problems of massive increases in population are now matched as common knowledge with the problems of pollution. There is growing concern about what is being poured into the atmosphere, the land, our rivers and the sea, and about the increase of dereliction. Ecology and conservation are not only fashionable words but also practical concepts to many more people than was the case even five years ago.

An increase in literature, books and articles, the effect of the Reith lectures in 1969 by Dr Fraser Darling and European Conservation Year have all had considerable impact in changing attitudes and making more people aware of the serious problems confronting man and his environment. There is the distinct possibility, unfortunately, that much of the thought and even publicity given to these aspects, though reaching an increasing number, has escaped the attention of the mass of the present population. However, one aspect has not passed the majority by—a progressive alteration in the stole and scope of leisure.

At the European Conservation Conference in Strasbourg in 1970 the rapporteur for the theme 'leisure' argued that 'leisure activity offered the most effective means of encouraging greater environmental awareness'. It is hardly necessary to point out that leisure can be used in an infinite variety of ways, many of which could have no connection with developing environmental awareness. Nevertheless, there is an increasing number of people using leisure time for visits to the countryside. These people might be classified as landscape viewers, since many of them choose not to move beyond their cars, or countryside ramblers who use the forest paths and streams as guide rails, or active participants who use the resources of the countryside or coast for activities or studies. There is every indication that the numbers in each of these groups will increase disproportionately to the inevitable increases in leisure time, disposable income, mobility and labour-saving devices.

As will be realized the problems which increased use of the countryside might be expected to produce have not gone unnoticed. How to solve the paradox of wanting to provide full use and maximum enjoyment for thousands, appreciating that through this there is the possibility of greater environmental awareness, while conserving the scarce resources is an absorbing problem.

EDUCATION AND LEISURE

Education plays its part in influencing this situation in several ways. The more educational opportunities there are for young people the more demand there is for recreational activity, and education also changes the direction of use of leisure. It seems certain that the more education a young person receives the more likely he is to seek active, purposeful leisure pursuits. If, therefore, we provide young people with a longer education and more relevant education in the use of their leisure, and particularly active recreation, then the numbers using the countryside will increase prodigiously. However, provision will not be enough, for not only will the demand for that increase but as James Fisher observed there will also be the necessity of considering the request for solitude for the masses as well. There can be no doubt of the necessity to prepare for and make positive use of these forecasts in order that an appreciation of the problems, as well as of the potential of the countryside, is built in to any likely influencing factor of education.

Having disposed for the moment of two of the most obvious connections between education and use of the countryside, namely leisure and conservation, it is time to look at the various approaches used by educators to introduce young people to the countryside for wide-ranging motives. Taking the view expressed by Dewey, that education is a process of living and not a preparation for future living, we subscribe to the opinion that through outdoor education there is the potential for educating young people in the broad sense as well as the specific, and that the education received will be of relevance at the time and will manifest itself, along with all the other aspects of education received at school, in later life in both expected and unexpected ways, depending upon individual development, circumstances and opportunity. It is likely that upon close analysis of the aims of all those involved in outdoor education the central theme would be living and learning out of doors, and it is in the development of this theme that variations occur.

APPROACHES TO OUTDOOR PURSUITS

The Outward Bound approach is one that deserves considerable recognition for its pioneering work in this field, and its importance can be judged from the acceptance of the idea by many who adapted it to their own situation.

Outward Bound courses were established to expose young people to a variety of experiences which would render them less vulnerable in times of hardship. They stemmed from the knowledge that young men were dying during the war through strain and physical hardship whilst older men were surviving, and in a way, continuation of the training given during the war could be justified in the light of increasing industrialization, technology and desk-bound education and work after the war had ended.

A report from the Devon Outward Bound school states: 'The main object is to develop the character through adventure afloat, in the mountains or through any medium where natural forces are present to produce the inspirations, challenges and obstacles essential to this experience.'

Kurt Hahn had of course prepared the ground for this sort of approach in his often quoted remark: 'It is culpable neglect not to impel young people into experiences.' Hogan in his book which uses Hahn's words in the title does add that it is necessary to stress that the young people exposed to these experiences must not only survive but should emerge strengthened. And, as Hahn regarded the foremost task of education 'to insure these qualities: an enterprising curiosity; an undefeatable spirit; tenacity in pursuit; readiness for self-denial; and, above all, compassion', it can be seen that the function of the Outward Bound schools was never to provide physical hardship for the sake of hardship as is often thought, but to try to put a range of testing experiences to young people in order that they could discover their personal reactions and limits, and at the same time affect attitudes and influence behaviour.

In a recent report on the Outward Bound movement it is stated that 'the aim of the schools is only incidentally to give a training in outdoor skills, but it is not surprising that students rate this aspect of the course highly since it is an obvious one, whilst character development is a much more subtle one'. And: 'The Trust is in the process of embarking upon entirely new ways of presenting established principles, and is considering quite dramatic experiments to widen the sphere within which Outward Bound operates.'

Such projects as City-Challenge, courses for executives, provision of courses for the handicapped and the place of Outward Bound in the requirements for added facilities upon the raising of the school leaving age no doubt come into this category. Due regard may well be given to an analysis undertaken at the Moray School of students' assessment of the values of a standard course:

1. The development of physical fitness and feeling of physical euphoria.
2. The learning of a new outdoor skill, such as climbing, or the improvement of a skill already partly learnt.

16

3. The overcoming of challenges or hazards and facing and mastering difficulties and problems.
4. The benefit from the discipline, or rather the voluntarily accepted training conditions, of no smoking or drinking.
5. The ability to work as a member of a team.
6. The ability to mix happily with all sorts of companions.
7. The increased sense of the needs of individuals, especially as realized through rescue activities and community service.
8. The individual help and supervision given by instructors.
9. The enjoyment of the countryside and appreciation of its beauty.
10. The mental development following from work done in discussion, projects and other intellectual or cultural pursuits.

There is probably a considerable amount of experience from Outward Bound schools in other parts of the world which could be utilized too. The American schools, for example, are not as concerned with industry as with the socialization and development of young people through contact with others from a wide variety of backgrounds in order to enable them to live in, work in and appreciate their society as a whole. Through experiences in the outdoors and all that is attached to the course it is hoped to influence young people's attitudes to such major issues as poverty, colour, love, human relationships and the development of mutual trust and respect between young people and adults. The Outward Bound development provides a very obvious example of the submergence of the activities by wider concepts and, as we have indicated, the use of the activities as vehicles for wider education is both legitimate and valuable.

Within the same theme is the observation of K. S. Pearce, a teacher at a school for maladjusted boys:

'I use the pursuits not as ends in themselves but as vehicles for the observation, diagnosis, treatment and testing of personality disorders shown by individuals. They constitute a group of activities which can serve to build up the self-confidence and social skills of the inadequate and unsocialized. Being largely non-intellectual they can be employed with a far wider range of children, including the school failures who cannot keep up with the pace of school work, and who therefore fail to identify with academic activities. Their unique usefulness would lie, if effective, largely in the education of the less sensitive, less imaginative, less academically able.'

This attitude that outdoor pursuits, in particular, should be reserved for the dull or difficult child is not uncommon and there is a great deal of evidence to suggest that success, or even just participation in the activities, has provided the key to fresh outlooks.

R. F. Mackenzie, head teacher of Braehead School in Fife, is reported to have asked Hamish Brown, the teacher in charge of outdoor pursuits: 'How would you like to take some boys to Glencoe and see what you can make of them? We can do little with them at school.'

At the same time, of course, it is possible to utilize the statement made by Senator Barry Goldwater that 'the use of the country-side as a means of developing academic achievement and individual responsibility is one of the most important steps taken in educa-tion'. This statement counteracts the impression that outdoor pursuits have more to offer the less able or the deprived boy or girl. On the contrary it is our firm belief that those of proven ability or from favoured backgrounds can benefit equally and should not themselves be deprived of the opportunities made available through outdoor pursuits. It will be realized that outdoor pursuits, though building up a considerable dossier of values, are not an educational panacea and that J. M. Hogan's words of caution might be well considered. 'What I want to say is that out-door pursuits have added to our educational armoury in a most significant way, but I think that it would be prudent for us to assume that we all have a great deal to learn about how most fruitfully they might be employed.'

We feel that we should document the more common uses to which outdoor pursuits are put before attempting to come to some conclusions. Quoting from the Lancashire Education Authority's camp school information sheet different dimensions again are added to those already outlined:

'We seek to provide a healthy outlook which will combat the tempta-tions that our highly civilized life affords. In a society which offers such safety and security the questing spirit of adventure must be provided for, and the challenge and comradeship which the hills and moors can offer is beyond doubt a rich alternative to the luxuries and easy pleasures of urban life. It is part of every child's heritage to know and understand his earth; to be at home in wild and magnificent places knowing how to find security and having confidence and ability to overcome obstacles. There is a spiritual value in the awesome splendour of the mountain scene and the humility of man.'

Statements such as these are clearly born out of a deep conviction and an absorption in the values of outdoor education for young people, and approach the sentiments and performances of many great people even in the modern world of mountains (Scott, Shackleton, Noyce, Hertzog, Rebuffat) and the sea (MacGregor, Chichester, Ridgeway). The poetic and spiritual aspects of work with young people are of great importance and it is interesting to read from a Braehead report: 'Many of our best outdoor boys and girls have gone on to scholastic heights. And how many others who would have resisted otherwise have come to accept reading and writing for pleasure and satisfaction.'

Braehead also indicates that one of the major values of outdoor education there is in job placement for the school leaver, and that it is not uncommon for those involved in outdoor education to go to work in forestry or on the land or join training courses for chefs.

The development of outdoor centres has of course opened the door to those who see residential experiences as valuable in themselves, especially for the city or town child, and that they provide considerable opportunity for aspects of social education. Many of the centres, established principally for outdoor pursuits, do not, as one might expect, have this same conviction. Twenty out of forty-two centres recently surveyed viewed the social effects of a stay as vital but incidental to the main task in hand, that of introducing young people to activities. There is certainly the need to clarify the aims of sending young people to centres and to staff and equip accordingly. Possibly the worst possible approach is to develop an activity or a facility and tack on new ideas without careful experiment and consultation. There are likely to be innumerable side benefits from young people staying in residential centres or on a camp or expedition together, but once again outdoor education does not contain all the answers, and it is felt that what it does contain or expand into should be educationally sound and born out of proven evidence and not intuition. It is interesting, for example, to compare the listed aims of a stay at an outdoor pursuits centre and at a field studies centre and amongst the latter note that the social advantages of a stay are often not mentioned!

The element of adventure is something which most people seriously engaged in outdoor pursuits would attempt to include in any programme. But adventure is often equated with danger rather than difficulty, and what some people call adventure really takes the form of an apology. Education authorities and those involved marginally in outdoor pursuits work do tend to resort to the explanation that everything new is an adventure to young people. This may be so, but often the young are capable of containing greater meaning within the concept of the word. 'Fear' is the essential component of adventure according to Colin Mortlock, lecturer in Outdoor Education at Charlotte Mason College, who certainly writes from experience and application. He describes adventures as 'the involvement in a situation which calls for all, or nearly all, a person's physical and mental resources to be utilized in surviving the situation'. Those who align their outdoor pursuits in this or a similar direction see that there is a heavy demand upon intelligence and not always on physical prowess, and that 'education for leisure' is an insufficient theme for young people. Challenge replaces competition, and capability substitutes for deliberate measures of success or failure. There is a great deal to be said for this approach, and it is supported by many young people themselves. Usually it is only advocated publicly by those who are sufficiently competent, well supported and equipped to be able to stand the rigours of placing young people in 'apparent' danger.

Northumberland Education Authority's approach is probably representative of a good number of LEAs. George Slee, Northumberland's Adviser in Outdoor Education, is of the opinion that

'the times might well not be far off when a child will leave school at 15+ with a fundamental understanding of the environment and of the need for its conservation; with the possession of skills which will allow his free movement and independence in the environment, together with experience of activities which will enable him to choose out of knowledge recreational pursuits to follow in his leisure time. Then the term outdoor education will have found real meaning and we shall be able to justify it as a viable concept and not merely an umbrella for a host of fragmented and unconnected approaches.'

Slee consideres the content of outdoor education to be threefold:

1. Field Studies—specific or general.

2. Expedition work.
3. Recreational activity.

Presumably the outcome being a balanced and related conservation and recreation awareness, which must be seen as a relevant school subject taking up curriculum time as well as maintaining voluntary effort by teachers. These are the very tangible aspects of outdoor education and relate closely to the requirements of our society and our environment; but by placing, for example, outdoor pursuits firmly in the recreational area there may well be the tendency to forgo many of the possibilities previously mentioned.

One of the ingredients that the Edinburgh Education Department incorporates into its programme is the belief that young people introduced to activities should be allowed every opportunity of achieving excellence, and this is, of course, the case in many other authorities. It is hoped, and expected, that some of the young people introduced to skiing, mountaineering, canoeing and sailing will represent their country at their chosen activity and that others will choose to participate in major expeditions or advanced work for its own sake. Edinburgh could, of course, be open to the criticism that it devotes all its attentions to the potentially good who may well be the socially or academically favoured as well. It can be countered, however, by the knowledge that Edinburgh caters for around 18 000 young people each year within countryside activity work and that it would be surprising if amongst this number some did not emerge as being interested or able enough to progress. We have chosen to outline some of the approaches and must reiterate that most people and authorities involved, particularly in outdoor pursuits make the most of opportunities, and that if their real goals remain constant their specific goals are always adaptable. The examples mentioned illustrate the wide range of approaches present throughout the country.

APPROACHES TO ENVIRONMENTAL STUDIES

Any description of the approaches to environmental studies will appear by comparison to the one on outdoor pursuits more formal, even more defined, but nevertheless equally wide ranging and possibly as confusing. Report Nine issued by the Council for Environmental Education contains the following statement:

21

'Confusion arises from the variable use of the term "environmental studies" sometimes as a synonym for environmental education, sometimes to describe a method of study within particular disciplines, and sometimes—as in this report—as the name of a new and developing subject in its own right.'

It would seem necessary to outline three areas which it might be considered relate to outdoor education before attempting to define the latter. The Schools Council Project started in 1967 in the primary school sector has produced the following guiding lines for those involved in environmental studies as,

'an approach through activities based on the child's physical and social environment which leads to the progressive development of attitudes and skills required for the observation, recording, interpretation and communication of scientific, historical and geographical data. The communication media required for such studies also necessitate an ever-increasing use of language and mathematics which are thereby, themselves, further developed. It is hoped that the end product will be children with a well-developed sense of inquiry and experiment, to whom has been brought an awareness of the intricacy and beauty that lie about them, and who have developed the means whereby to observe and communicate through a wide variety of skills.'

Once again, although teachers and authorities have arrived at a central theme, there is wide disparity in methods and results. In schools it is possible to experience the following all under the guise of environmental studies:

1. The study of a local topic for a short period of time either within one subject or possibly utilizing the resources of a number, e.g. geography, history or science.
2. The accumulation of information from books, films or lectures which has little relevance if conducted without direct reference to the area under discussion.
3. The development of skills, collection, identification, analysis, reporting.
4. Scientific examination of a locality as a base for wider concentric studies, using the skills developed.
5. The integrated day based on the environment, e.g. the sea shore, forestry.
6. Use of a field study centre once a year, usually away from the school.

7. The establishment of day centres where constant examination of a study area can be achieved and which leads to a progression in the work undertaken.

Environmental studies as an educational area seems to divide into two quite readily without creating a situation where the two parts are incompatible. The scientific part is quite specific in its aims, i.e. skills, providing a sound base for learning and sequential study. The general part, which to be educationally sound must surely be progressive too, can be more concerned with individual reactions to situations, the creative use of resources and the development of concentric ideas springing out of opportunity and enthusiasm, e.g. the production of models, paintings, handwork, written passages and local projects combining a variety of subject matter. The National Rural and Environmental Studies Association in 1970 defined their areas as: 'The study of the landscape; its topography, geology and pedology; the ecological relationship of the plants and animals naturally present, together with the study of man's control of the natural environment through agriculture, horticulture and forestry.'

The main objective of the Association, however, is to 'promote an understanding of the countryside and of man's relation to the natural environment and to wild life', and recognize that environment includes the 'urban scene' as well as the 'rural'. Here again we have a combined approach—the understanding and conservation aspect being moulded into the scientific approach. Environmental education 'is the process of recognizing values and clarifying concepts in order to develop skills and attitudes necessary in order to understand and appreciate the inter-relatedness of man, his cultural and his biophysical surroundings. Environmental education also entails practice in decision making and self-formulation of a code of behaviour about issues concerning environmental quality', according to the International Working Party on Environmental Education on the school curriculum. It was agreed at this conference that environmental education is a science-centred, multi-disciplinary subject where most if not all school subjects could and should be incorporated and the requirements were as follows:

1. Appropriate education at pre-school level.
2. Teaching of environmental conservation in schools, colleges and universities.

23

3. The teaching and training of specialists in conservation and management in schools and universities.
4. Out of school education, through activities, of children, young people and adults.
5. Dissemination of environmental conservation ideas and principles among the broad general public.

So it could be considered that environmental education comes down firmly on the side of a scientific approach to conservation education and training. However, many teachers involved in environmental education for all pupils would see the importance of it in the following ways:

1. First-hand experience in the field of the natural environment, which to be effective must be carefully planned and organized with adequate preparation and completion time built in.
2. The discovery of inter-relationships in the physical, cultural and scientific environments.
3. An appreciation, through awareness and understanding, of the natural environment and its problems and potential for leisure, conservation, economic and human use.
4. At school level there is the undoubted possibility of bringing young people together through environmental study in the field and educating them in social, physical and moral attitudes acceptable to themselves and the community.

These are remarkably similar aims in essence when compared with the aims of outdoor pursuits, and it is of course this bringing together which is one of the pure functions of outdoor education.

It is worth recording some of the findings of an investigation into the value of field study to pupils of 11–15 years old conducted by Dr J. Clarke. He found for the group he tested that:

1. In all cases tested, and for every test given, the outdoor classes were superior to the corresponding indoor classes.
2. The ability to write biological answers in good lucid English is enhanced by field study.
3. The pupils found the work pleasurable, they conducted themselves more co-operatively, they discussed their work more freely and they worked harder.
4. While field work appears to be conducive to learning for all pupils tested, the younger ones (11–13 years) derive more

benefit from it than the older ones. It is interesting to note that age seems to be a bigger factor than environment or social class.

This less scientific, more educational approach, aiming at providing a grounding in a variety of aspects, is probably one which has the most significant part to play for all kinds of young people, and it is certainly this approach which is more akin to the thinking behind the development of outdoor education.

Perhaps the Field Studies Council can be thought of as the counterpart of the Outward Bound Trust in the sense that it too was an innovator and continues to examine its own role critically. The council's recent report claims that

'its work has expanded in step with the growth of fresh concepts in educational theory; a new appreciation of the value of first-hand data in science teaching, a recognition of biology as a gateway to science, the coming of age of geography as a bridging discipline and the realization of man's urgent need to understand his environment better. Many teachers have adopted field work on its own merits; others have done so under the pressure of changing examination syllabus.'

In the past field studies have been principally associated with that part of a subject which necessitated specific study, usually for examination purposes. However, those involved in field studies are beginning to add further dimensions to even these specific studies in the way of, usually, conservationist principles. Having looked at these approaches it is interesting to return to the report of the Council for Environmental Education (1971) and read that

'the Council notes with satisfaction the growing recognition of the essential unity or wholeness of environmental education seen no longer as the exclusive prerogative of any one subject. As an educational approach, it can permeate a range of disciplines both traditional and new as well as form the mainspring of many integrated courses. With its objectives and methodology firmly inter-related it can impart the balanced understanding of and active concern for the whole environment which alone can enable man to plan and realize a world fit to live in.'

It is not really the purpose of this book to express firm opinions on what can or should be achieved in education, but perhaps we could record our belief that 'conservation education' is identical in concept to 'leisure education', and that the justification for attempting to introduce these areas as specific unrelated school subjects seems suspect. It is our opinion that both of these aspects would be better served as integral parts of general education leading to personal decision making, on how to increase understanding and skills, to use, appreciate and enjoy the countryside, and also, for example, the arts, literature, television, home decorating and parenthood.

What is noticeable from our brief outline of the approaches to use of the environment is the lack of mention of outdoor pursuits. At the Education in the Countryside Conference at Keele in 1965 there was no specific mention of outdoor pursuits, and nor were there representatives of that field except for those from Brathay Hall, the Youth Hostel Association and the Duke of Edinburgh Award Scheme. Just recently Philip Oswald, Head of the Nature Conservancy's Education Department, wrote: 'Many of the exponents of outdoor pursuits have shown little interest in nature conservation, though some were prominent in the movement which pressed for the establishment of National Parks.'

No doubt it could be said that those involved in introducing young children to the countryside through environmental study have had neither the skill nor the interest in introducing young people to activities. However, it would seem to us that upon careful observation it is likely that a great deal of combined work has been undertaken, especially by teachers and club leaders. There is scope for more of this, and what is required is an approach to the outdoors which is aimed to suit the young person, taking into account his other commitments, his energies and enthusiasms.

OUTDOOR EDUCATION

Our definition of outdoor education stems from this belief, and is succinctly stated by the National Association for Outdoor Education as 'a means of approaching educational objectives through guided direct experience in the outdoors; using as learning material the resources of the countryside and coastline'. This means in effect that outdoor education contains within it a combination of outdoor pursuits and studies in the rural environment, but that it is not necessary for them to be practised simultaneously or even in proportion to one another. However, as there is a wide expanse of common ground between the two it is, in our opinion, both wasteful to keep the two totally apart and almost impossible. It is in some ways surprising that in many education authorities a greater emphasis and more facilities have been allocated to outdoor pursuits than to environmental studies; and yet the latter has had the advantage of remaining within the main stream of education, and teachers have been adequately trained to pursue this work with pupils. As has been shown, the fundamental aims of these two aspects are very much the same. It would seem to us that without losing either its identity or its distinctive contribution there could emerge a synthesis of many of the facets of each to forge greater links between them, which avoids the wasteful effect of duplication, eradicates the problems and produces a valuable medium for the education of all pupils regardless of their social or academic standing. We are aware that we are advocating using the environment as a medium for education which will allow for such concepts as aesthetic and ethical values to be incorporated as well as social effects, skill and study training and enjoyment to be included. Whilst purely scientific study and the preservation of a suitable environment and the provision of opportunities for leisure must also be the concern of education it is felt that they should be incorporated into general education or integrated into appropriate subjects. In an article in *Education* in 1970 Terry Parker wrote:

'Paradoxically, both the strength and weakness of Outdoor Education lie in the fact that it is not a school discipline in the accepted sense. It has no absolutely distinctive core of knowledge nor even a specific structure; its formation springs from a lengthy list of practical and educational objectives. Outdoor Education can therefore be categorized as a "subject" of opportunity. The objectives are best achieved in such areas as the coast, islands, hills, caves, rivers, isolated countryside, nature reserves and forests, but the initial experience can lead to many new and differing explorations, situations and accomplishments.'

There are signs that the objectives of outdoor education are becoming clearer, that its content is no longer vague, and an examination of the historical developments of environmental studies and outdoor pursuits indicates a relevant structure is emerging.

BIBLIOGRAPHY

ARVILL R. *Man and Environment.* Pelican, 1969.

BARR J. *Derelict Britain.* Pelican, 1969.

CLARKE J. H. An Investigation into the Value of Field Studies to Pupils of 11–15 years old. *School Science Review* No. 49, 1967.

CLAWSON M. & KNETSCH J. L. *Economics of Outdoor Recreation.* John Hopkins, 1967.

FLETCHER B. A. *Outward Bound—A Follow up Study.* Dept of Education, Bristol University, 1970.

HOGAN J. M. *Impelled into Experience.* Educational Productions Ltd, 1968.

NICHOLSON M. *The Environmental Revolution.* Hodder and Stoughton, 1970.

PATMORE A. *Land and Leisure.* David & Charles, 1970.

Annual Report 1969–70. Field Studies Council.

Council for Environmental Education Report No. 9.

Curriculum Development Project on Environmental Studies. Schools Council Report, 1970.

International Union for Conservation of Nature and Natural Resources. *Environmental Education—The School Curriculum.* UNESCO, 1970.

Leisure. European Conservation Conference Report. Strassbourg, 1970.

National Association for Outdoor Education Conference Report, 1971.

Using the Environment—Nature Conservancy Report, 1969.

Outward Bound Schools Annual Reports. Outward Bound Trust.

Significant events and developments within the concept of outdoor education

At the same time that Robert Lowe was observing that he believed 'it would be necessary to compel our future masters to learn their letters' there was the not unrelated concern to provide the population with additional facilities, and to introduce measures which would ensure provision and protection of natural resources.

It is not surprising to detect in the historical progress of both outdoor pursuits and environmental studies similar patterns of action. First of all there can be traced the enlightened views of certain people epitomized perhaps by Wordsworth's suggestion, in 1810, that the Lake District ought to be national property. Then follows the work of schools and informal bodies and normally more organized development leading to memoranda and finally legislation. The length of time that all of this takes varies considerably, but some idea of the possible scale is given when we find that it was not until 1951 that the Lake District did, in fact, become a National Park.

We have chosen to look at environmental studies and outdoor pursuits separately and to outline national development, which it will be seen had some impact on the gradual growth of attention which is now being given to outdoor education.

In 1851 half of England's population could be described as urban dwellers, and it was around this time that museums and libraries, arboretums and public gardens were first provided in any quantity. The year 1860 saw the first of the urban parks, though it was not until ten years later that the Bank Holiday Act gave working people the right to a half-day per week and four days' holiday per year which enabled them to use the new provisions in any great measure. However, Wordsworth's concern for the future of the Lake District illustrated that there was a considerable number of people, mainly middle class, using the countryside for their leisure and anxious that it was cared for appropriately. In 1883 the Lake District Defence Society was organized, and this led in 1895 to the formation of the National Trust for Places of Historic Interest and Natural Beauty with its first site at Dinas Olen, a cliff near Barmouth in North Wales. The Royal Society for the Protection of Birds had already been formed in 1889, so it can be seen that towards the end of the nineteenth century there were quite clear examples of the evolution of the pattern.

By 1911 the proportion of urban dwellers in England had increased to 80 per cent. Though the forest parks are a fairly recent concept the Forestry Commission was established in 1919, and the next decade saw the beginning of the first Country Naturalist Trusts. Norfolk provided the first in 1926, and this was also the year of the foundation of the Council for the Preservation of Rural England. It is worth bearing in mind that even at this time there were only 1.5 million workers with paid holidays, and that it was not until just prior to the outbreak of the 1914–18 war that the Holidays with Pay Act was introduced. It is relevant to insert, though not to elaborate upon, at this juncture the fact that 1940 was the year of the founding of the Youth Hostel Association.

Lindsey County Council's initiative resulted in the Sandhills Act in 1930, which was obviously intended to control any misuse of the dunes and surrounding areas. This fact may be construed as one of the first examples of the extension of the pattern from fairly formal voluntary work to legislation, but it was not until after the war that the first major example can be found.

The Town and Country Planning Act came into being in 1947, and one of its functions was 'to define and propose areas of Great Landscape, Historic or Scientific Value'. It was followed two years later by the National Parks and Access to the Countryside Act, which enabled a National Parks Commission to be formed. Part of the Act called for 'the preservation and enhancement of natural beauty and the provision of opportunities for open-air recreation and the study of nature'. From this short extract it can be realized how significant this Act was to prove. The commission can be said to be responsible for features which we recognize easily today. The national parks originated and expanded in number, though it was not until 1966 that the Peak Park received the European Diploma from the Council of Europe. Areas of outstanding natural beauty were added to those of great landscape, historic or scientific value, and the need for nature reserves and long-distance footpaths was given recognition. Legislation having paved the accepted way, the development of the pattern was speeded up by what might be described as the professional approach closely linked to the work of the established groups.

The Nature Conservancy was created in 1949 and in 1965 became part of the Natural Environment Research Council. The years 1957 and 1958 saw the European Information Centre for Nature Conservation opened and the International Council for Nature functioning. Over fifty nature trails were introduced during National Nature Week in 1963 and in this year the first of the Countryside in '70 Conferences was held. The second was in 1965, coinciding with the formation of the Sports Council arising in part from the Wolfenden Committee's report five years before.

A major landmark can be attributed to 1968 when the Countryside Act became effective. Through this Act the Countryside Commissions replaced the National Parks Commission, though sections of the new charter are very reminiscent of those important directives of 1949. For example, 'regard must be paid to the desirability of conserving the natural beauty and amenity of the countryside' and 'of providing, or improving, opportunities for the enjoyment of the countryside by the public'.

It would be quite wrong to give the impression that only these major events were of significance in supporting or altering attitudes and actions. The increase in nature trails, the ranger service in national parks, the creation of focal points like Slimbridge or the Osprey Observatory at Loch Garten, or Landmark, the interpretative centre at Carrbridge in the Cairngorms, exemplify the increasing awareness of using the countryside's resources positively. A good example of this trend is provided by the Forestry Commission, the largest land holders in Britain.

'The Commission has already been active in providing the recreational use of its forests. It has seven picnic places, two hundred and one forest trails and three scenic forest drives for motorists. Other facilities include information centres, observation towers and wildlife museums.

Over fifteen million day visits were made to these facilities in 1970 and some one million campers made use of the camping sites.'

Of necessity one has also to take into account, when trying to assess the overall situation, the expansion of other aspects which affect the environment of which the countryside is part. Refineries and oil discharge installations, hydro-electric power stations, reactor sites, radio masts, new roads, caravan sites and incidents like the *Torrey Canyon* disaster require equal attention in pursuing this picture. In this area it is not unexpected to find a comparable pattern to that outlined previously. The 1955 Road Verge Agreement was formulated by the Nature Conservancy and the Ministry of Transport. The Transport Acts of 1962 and 1968 resulted in the closing of railway lines with considerable repercussions and scope for creating linear routes for walkers, cyclists and horse riders, and the opportunity to develop the long neglected and wasting asset of the British canal system with its great potential for water- and land-based recreation.

If nothing else European Conservation Year 1970 served to highlight a great number of these facilities as well as contributing a great deal to the knowledgeable use of the countryside.

It should not go unmentioned that research reports, surveys and planning papers have all played a significant part in documenting and providing information and relevant advice on which knowledgeable action can be based. Lastly, and to add another dimension to the pattern, the creation of a Ministry of the Environment can be seen as an appropriate accolade to the progress made during the last one hundred years.

The major concern of this book is with education, but it is our contention that the development of educational practices cannot, or should not, be seen in isolation. The role of education in influencing the use of the countryside is now being recognized more fully, and it would be true to say that educationalists are becoming more adept at using the countryside.

The formation in 1968 and 1969 of the Council for Environmental Education (England and Wales) and the Committee on Education and the Countryside (Scotland) is as significant as the Countryside Act itself. Sir Jack Longland at the Countryside in '70 Conference in 1963 observed that

'this [use of the outdoors by teachers] is becoming something much bigger than the recreational use of the countryside. It is becoming an accepted part of the education of boys and girls that this part of education outside and beyond the classroom in wild country should be regarded as a perfectly normal bit of schooling.'

It is necessary now to explore both the reasons and the landmarks which caused Longland to express this opinion, and to relate this to the historical data already outlined. Once again we feel that it is helpful to look at environmental studies and outdoor pursuits separately, though not in isolation.

THE DEVELOPMENT OF ENVIRONMENTAL STUDIES IN EDUCATION

Evolution rather than revolution is a formula which is dear to the hearts of many involved even in innovation in education. Use of the environment immediately surrounding the school and visiting areas away from the vicinity are recent changes in the range of educational practices.

Despite Lowe's belief that education was essential in order to produce a meaningful franchise after the second Reform Act of 1867, it is only in this century that elaboration on the originally narrow insistence on basic skills has been achieved. Educational philosophers and practitioners (chief of whom were Dewey, Froebel and Montessori) caused considerable reappraisal of both the style and content of teaching in the first ten years of the 1900s.

The 1904 Balfour Education Act had, unfortunately, advocated a continuance of a narrow education, but there was to be immediate reaction to this policy and a growing movement began to produce smaller classes, improve the relationships between teachers and pupils, and to formulate a realistic and humane teaching pattern which took into account the interests of individual children. These innovations had profound effects upon the elementary school system and began the diversification and liberalization of the curriculum. The development continued with the work of such people as Decroly and Piaget, and it is to these beginnings that work beyond the confined scope of the classroom can be traced.

Other influences affecting the growth of the use of the countryside will be described in the section outlining the development of outdoor pursuits, but briefly they stemmed from the beliefs and

33

practices of the British public school and from Germany and Sweden. It was to these influences in particular that the opening of the first British Youth Hostel in 1930 can be attributed.

Particular mention must be made at this point of the conributtion of the uniformed voluntary organizations, and in particular of the Scouts. Since 1907 the Scouts and Guides through their badge systems had been encouraging young people to camp, hillwalk and generally to use the countryside for exploration and, at the same time, become aware of and preserve its many facilities.

The emergence of such movements serves to illustrate both the demand and the background of a growing awareness of some of the potentiality of the countryside. The Hadow Report (Report of the Consultative Committee on the Primary School) contained no mention of environmental studies as such, but the recommendation that teaching should be concerned with activity and experiences for young children rather than solely with the transmission of facts and skills was most appropriate to the sections which the report did contain on geography, history and nature study.

Nature study remained as the title for the large part of the growing number of projects and excursions arranged by schools prior to the war, though in some instances this was replaced, or augmented, by rural studies and the acquisition of facilities for gardening and farming on school sites.

In 1941 the Norwood Report contained the following statement, that it was essential 'to bring boys and girls in touch with sea and mountain and in open air tasks and ventures to build up the moral strength which comes from such contact'.

The camp schools were used for evacuees, but restored to their original purpose after 1945, and these facilities were added to by the first of the Field Studies Council's Centres at Flatford Mill in 1946. The Field Studies Council, a private body with no official funds, was originated in 1943 and it has added nine other centres to its ranks. It is significant to record that now over 60 per cent of the total visitors to these centres are from schools.

The late 1940s produced two important Acts, the Town and Country Planning Act and the National Parks and Access to the Countryside Act. These, coupled with relevant attainments in the educational sector, might well serve to illustrate the very real beginnings of converging relations between naturalist and educationalists resulted in the following statement made by the Nature Conservancy in its Annual Report of 1959, causing little dissent: 'The key to informing the general public about nature conservation must lie with the schools.'

Another link can be seen in the formation of the Conservation Corps through the auspices of the International Council for Nature.

The Conservation Corps is a charitable organization and its function is:

1. To assist in the management of nature reserves and other biologically important sites using voluntary labour.
2. To educate its volunteers in the principles and practices of nature conservation.

The report of the Crowther Committee, which looked into the problems of the fifteen to eighteen age range in 1959, gave ample recognition to the value of the Outward Bound schools, Brathay Hall and the Duke of Edinburgh Award Scheme, and their role is more appropriately detailed in the next section.

In the schools the way was being paved for rather more dynamic changes by the steady increase in in-service training for teachers in the use of the environment and by the work of the Nuffield Foundation, leading via the Junior Science Project to the establishment of the Environmental Studies Curriculum Development Project based in Wales and Shropshire. This project originally involved seventy schools under the Schools Council, which had been formed in 1964 and which assumed responsibility for the work previously carried out by the former Secondary Schools Examinations Council and the Curriculum Study Group.

Environmental study projects have been included in the work of the Council and these will be placed in context later.

The extensive sharpening of interest and action in the early and mid 1960s is reflected, indirectly perhaps, in several major educational reports of the same time. Newsom (1963) placed emphasis on residential experience, especially for the average and less than average pupil, and supported a variety of undertakings listed amongst outdoor pursuits, Duke of Edinburgh Award activities and field studies. It is unfortunate that many of these activities then became associated with the 'less than average pupil', and in this sense the Newsom Report, and the Brunton Report relating to Scotland, published in the same year, can be considered to have proved of disservice.

However, contained in the Newsom Report was the following: 'Most, however, of these undertakings have important features in common. By introducing boys and girls to fresh surroundings and helping them to acquire new knowledge or try their hand at fresh skills they provide a general educational stimulus,' and in the Brunton Report there was a demand for 'some understanding of the environment'. Both of these reports voiced opinions on the unsuitability of water-tight compartments encouraged by single-subject teaching, and Newsom, when considering what should be included in the modern school curriculum, supported an extension of what was then known as rural science.

Reports on the primary schools also contained comment and advice on teaching through the environment. The memorandum 'Primary Education in Scotland' (1965) called for the necessity of 'fostering an interest in and understanding of the environment of Man'. The document 'Children and their Primary Schools', produced by the Plowden Committee in 1966, contained several appropriate references:

'Nearly all children are interested in living forms whether they be animal or plant. Some acquaintance with them is an essential part of being educated.'

'Another effective way of integrating the curriculum is to relate it through the use of the environment to the boundless curiosity which children have for the world about them.'

Plowden also pointed out the advisability of involving rural children in exploration of the countryside as well as their urban counterparts and the help authorities could give by providing residential centres. Certainly by 1966 a number of education authorities had provided centres normally geographically detached from the base and perhaps more inclined to concentrate on activity and the social gains of residential experience. The work being done in schools and at these centres was described in considerable detail with far-reaching effect at two conferences in 1965. In March 1965 at the Conference on Education in the Countryside at Keele University the delegates concluded that:

1. Positive educational methods are needed to encourage aware-

ness and appreciation of the natural environment as well as responsibility for its trusteeship by every citizen.
2. The educational system has a decisive contribution to make in creating this awareness and sense of individual responsibility.
3. The countryside is a rich source of inspiration and teaching material which can contribute substantially to education at all levels; field studies provide a valuable mean sof using and developing this educational resource.
4. If properly integrated into the curriculum field studies can form a valuable part of the whole school course. They provide an opportunity of relating many subjects more directly to the natural environment and of fostering a deeper understanding of the forces affecting it.

The Conference on Field Studies at Residential Centres in November 1965 convened by the Field Studies Council contributed in like manner, and the combined resolutions proved to be those accepted by the 'Countryside in 1970' second conference in 1965.

Perhaps of equal importance was the role that all these conferences played in bringing together formally representatives from education authorities, statutory and voluntary bodies, causing increased impetus in countryside studies and joint projects springing out of a knowledge of each other's role and aims. The Hedgerow Project was the result of co-operation by schools with the Nature Conservancy; the Rights of Way Survey with the Countryside Commission; the Adoption of Forest Plots with the Forestry Commission; and so on.

Definite awareness of each other's contribution had become more prevalent in the late 1950s, more formal links were now being forged, and, for the present, the culmination of this process was the formation of the Council for Environmental Education (England and Wales) and the Committee for Education in the Countryside (Scotland). Perhaps of some significance is the fact that the secretariat for the former was originally provided by the Education Advisory Section of the Nature Conservancy and for the latter by the Countryside Commission for Scotland. It should be added at this point that the Royal Society for the Protection of Birds had for some time been strong supporters of the necessity for providing meaningful information for schools and children.

The programme of the European Conservation year, with its themes of information and interpretation of the countryside, helped to strengthen the links between all those involved in management, use and conservation and produced more projects. National newspapers like the *Guardian* became involved and the Youth Hostels Association ran a national competition in Scotland, but the great number of local or regional enterprises was equally impressive. Of course, not all the projects were successful, and some ironically failed because of over enthusiasm—not many seemed to fail because of lack of support.

Not surprisingly the veritable explosion of young people being involved in countryside activity and study causes problems, and even in 1968 it was felt necessary to produce an Outdoor Studies Code complementary to the basic Country Code, and in 1970 the Royal Geographical Society published a memorandum warning against, in particular, over visiting and over collecting from countryside resources.

Alongside all the general development is an awareness of the potential of the countryside as a vehicle for education in its widest sense, physical, social, academic, and in its more narrow sense of promoting a sense of responsibility for the future of the countryside, there has been a movement by some to gain recognition for environmental studies because of its own intrinsic, usually scientific, value. This has involved the growth of curriculum work and of examination at all levels with all that those aspects of education entail.

The previous chapter contained an outline of the claims of this movement, and the only addition made here is in fact its place chronologically. It must be emphasized once again that this book is concerned mainly with countryside studies, which we see as part of the system which includes environmental studies and field studies. Our concern for the preservation of this sort of study alongside outdoor pursuits is not our sole preoccupation, as perhaps can be indicated by the formation of the National Association for Outdoor Education in 1970. Furthermore, the natural interaction of the two aspects, as we have begun to outline, is invaluable if we are to attempt to reach the mass of our schoolchildren who have no academic expectations or expertise in botany, geology, archaeology or natural history, and who are otherwise unlikely to hear of such agencies as the Countryside Commission, the Nature Conservancy, the National Trust or the Junior Ornithologists.

The Committe on Education in the Countryside in a publication stated that 'the variety of outdoor pursuits, increasing both in scope and impact upon pupils, can stimulate and provide opportunities for developing an interest in environmental studies'.

It is now time to look at the historical development of outdoor pursuits, and trace in the educational area the change of emphasis from skill learning to a much broader approach, encompassing a responsible attitude towards the countryside.

THE DEVELOPMENT OF OUTDOOR PURSUITS IN EDUCATION

The many different names which are used to describe what are essentially the same group of physical activities serves to complicate what should be a very simple situation. For many years, and in particular since the middle 1950s, physical educationalists have been moving inexorably towards a wider acceptance of outdoor activities as an integral part of the physical education provision in Britain. The term 'outdoor pursuits' is used perhaps no more frequently than any of those listed in the introduction, 'adventure training', 'open country pursuits' or Outward Bound; each places a slightly different emphasis on the purpose of the activity but it is the activity itself which concerns us here. The term 'outdoor pursuits' is perhaps the most general and it will therefore be necessary to define it, since the term will be used throughout the book. Outdoor pursuits are necessarily physically demanding undertakings performed outside the classroom or lecture theatre. The activities include those which rely more on the natural environment than on artificial situations and for which overt competition is not an essential feature. This is still a very wide field and would cover activities ranging from skindiving and swimming to gliding and cycling. The field is narrowed a little by admitting the element of danger which is implied in 'adventure training'. The most common of the outdoor activities are therefore walking, camping, sailing, skiing, canoeing, climbing and caving. This does not imply that pony trekking and camping are devoid of hazard (Fig. 13), but both in the public imagination and in the accident statistics they are relatively safe sports. Why is it that these 'outdoor pursuits' have assumed an important position, are occupying considerable thought in the minds of educationalists, and are, year by year, demanding a greater share of the financial budget of the physical education allowance in the schools, colleges and universities of Britain? A movement such as this cannot appear like a mushroom overnight; and it is necessary to examine the historical traditions of physical education in Britain, and examine these in the changing context of British society, to be able to offer an adequate explanation for the present phenomenon. As in any movement there must be an established need for development or redeployment of facilities. The history of physical education, like any other facet of education, not only in Britain but throughout the world has reflected the needs of society. Until the scientific and technological revolution of the present century, physical prowess was equated with military strength, and it is no surprise that the earliest physical training was directed towards this end. In Britain it is possible to trace the development of physical education through the nationalistic military phase to a period of remedial gymnastics, and finally to the present unambiguous emphasis on physical recreation. Although the trend has always been present, changing circumstances of society and national needs have inevitably caused occasional reversals.

From the sixteenth century progressive educationalists such as Roger Ascham, J. R. Vives and Richard Mulcaster were aware of the development potential of physical education, but in spite of their encouragement the social climate did not provide an opportunity for wide-scale participation in physical education. The patriotic fervour which gave rise to the German school of gymnastics in the period between 1775 and 1850, and the popularization of physical education which was the inevitable outcome, had a profound effect on attitudes in Britain. The importance which was attributed to physical education, and in particular to the games-playing tradition which had developed in the private sector of British education during the eighteenth and nineteenth centuries, found favour in the 1864 report of the Clarendon Commission. As a result of this report the Education Act of 1870 made provision for physical education and games periods; by 1895 Sir Edward Chadwick's campaign resulted in the inclusion of physical drill as a prerequisite for obtaining a school grant.

A distinct dichotomy in physical education provision existed at the beginning of this century with a definite emphasis on military drill for boys and the introduction of the new Swedish gymnastics for girls. The girls' gymnastics required new teachers trained in these skills; their training was conducted through a number of women's colleges established between 1878 and 1898. Credit for the widespread dissemination of Swedish gymnastics must go to the Cross Commission which, in 1888, recommended this form of training for girls in all elementary schools. The commission failed, however, to make a revised provision for the physical education of boys, and it was not until after the First World War that a liberalizing element was generally effective.

Throughout Britain there were, of course, regional variations in the interpretation of the value of some aspects of physical education. In Wales, for example, games were widely repressed by the Methodist revival of the late eighteenth and early nineteenth centuries. They held the view that the playing of games, even on weekdays, was levity and was inconsistent with the seriousness of life.

In the changing social context of the nineteenth century youth itself took an increasing part in determining its own destiny. To a large extent this trend was brought about on the one hand by a direct conflict between the philosophy of the romantic writers such as Tieck, Novalis, Arnim and Rousseau, who fostered an appreciation of folk culture and the natural beauty of the countryside, and on the other the growing squalor of urban industrialization and the insistence of the academic grind, particularly in the German gymnasia.

The ideals of the early youth movements often reflected the ideals of the adult society under whose patronage they were usually directed. As in wider educational fields the needs and aspirations of society determined the orientation of youth groups. The first youth groups began to appear in the 1880s and were based on Christian principles. Typical of these was the Boys Brigade, founded by Sir William Smith in 1883.

Drawing his members from among the working class in Glasgow, his ideal of Christianity, tempered with military discipline, had a strong appeal. The success of the movement was such that in 1943 King George VI, as their patron, was able to say that Smith had 'builded better than he knew, for he started not only a great movement but one from which all our present widespread youth

41

training was destined to spring'. In Germany the birth of the youth movement was rather more autonomous; inspired by Karl Fischer, a student at the Steglitz Gymnasium, German youth sought recognition as a community in its own right instead of merely being considered as an uneasy and frustrating interlude between childhood and maturity. This was the *raison d'être* of the Wandervogel which was founded in 1901. Its purpose was not only to provide cheap holidays in the country, but to provide self-education through self-reliance and communal activities. In order to cater for the demands of inexpensive accommodation the Wandervogel established a number of Landheime; by 1913 there were 640 such hostels. In Britain the need for this type of accommodation was almost as pressing, but it was not until 1930, however, that the Youth Hostel Association was founded in Britain to satisfy its demand. The growth of the movement during the period to the Second World War was very rapid; alternative forms of accommodation, and in particular the rise in popularity of camping, meant that after the war the movement failed to increase, and from 1950 there has even been a slight decline in the number of hostels open (Fig. 1).

By the end of the nineteenth century the principle of an annual holiday was becoming widely accepted, and the revolution in communications brought about by the railway network made it possible for the first time for large numbers to take their holiday away from home. In 1891 T. A. Leonard founded the Co-operative Holidays Association (CHA) and has been called the father of the open-air movement. Another great movement, the Boy Scouts, founded in 1908 by Baden Powell, quickly caught the imagination of both young people and educationalists throughout Europe. By 1911 the Wandervögel had reached such proportions with so many specialized and local sections that Rust, Minister of Education, pressed all the gymnastic clubs to unite for the good of the physical development of German youth. Before the First World War political unrest in Germany manifested itself in extreme views, views which were reflected in the political orientation of the youth groups. During the period between the wars the Verband für Deutsche Jugendherbergen (German Youth Hostels Association) continued to grow in response to the continuing demands of the youth club groups. The increase in hostels between 1919 and 1927 was from 300 to over 2 000. The extent of interest expressed

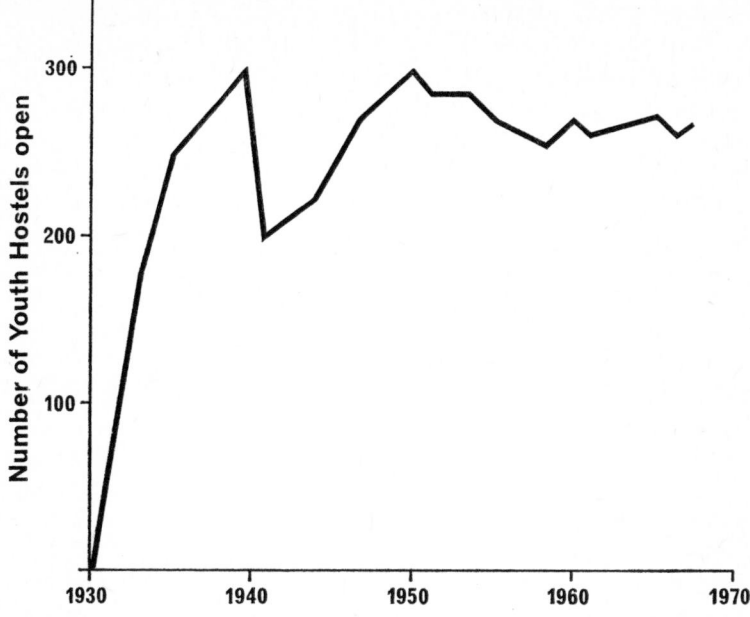

Figure 1   The growth of the youth hostel movement in Britain between 1930–70.

in these educational opportunities is most clearly seen in the Hitler Jugend and Band Deutsche Maedel for whom it was intended to provide fifty thousand training centres by 1943. The whole of the educational system was geared to the National Socialist Party and consequently Rust, the Minister of Education, placed a strong emphasis on physical training, which was compulsory in all schools throughout the whole of each afternoon. Although one is tempted to criticize the motive behind these provisions, it was from the ideals of the early youth movements that educationalists were inspired to experiment with less rigid forms of physical education.

Impressed by the intellectual excellence of the German secondary schools, and strongly influenced by the philosophy of John Ruskin and French Romanticism, Dr Cecil Reddie founded Abbotsholme School in 1889. The school attempted to develop both body and mind in pleasant surroundings and to inculcate a sense of social responsibility through communal work. Hermann Leitz was a member of the staff in 1896, and on returning to Germany he found little difficulty in establishing a similar school in the same unsettled social environment which gave rise to the Wandervogel. The first of his Landerziehungheime was opened at Ilsenberg in 1889 and was followed by Haubinda in 1901 and Biberstein in der Rhon in 1904. These schools inspired a wide range of experimental schools both in the private sector and under Weimar government. Referring to these schools, Professor Alexander wrote: 'There is a tinge of paganism in the philosophy of the Gemeinschaft Schulen, for they return to nature with enthusiasm that accepts all she offers as good and holy. This swing towards naturalism is part of the revolt against conventions that accompanied the youth movements.'

Articles 142–50 of the Weimar constitution actively encouraged the principles of the Schulwandering (school journey) and the Wander Tag (expedition day)—indeed the whole of the Mittelschule syllabus offered progressive training in expedition work culminating in fifteen-mile hikes. Many of the more ambitious schools established their own Schullandheime (school expedition centres). In describing the foundation of Salem School in 1919, Kurt Hahn freely admits that he evolved his educational philosophy from many sources: from Plato, from Dr Arnold of Rugby, from Eton, from Hermann Leitz, from Fichte and Wilhelm Meister. Although he was drawing on the traditions of the British public schools, he did not overemphasize the importance of games. When he was forced to leave Germany in 1934 it is no surprise that he should have established Gordonstoun on lines similar to those that he had worked out at Salem. Hahn felt that the ravages of peace were no less important than the ravages of war; peace too often bred an attitude of indolence and indifference which, in the past, only war had been able to dispel. He was convinced that the arduous challenges offered by the mountains and sea could provide a peaceful and acceptable medium through which a person's character might be trained. In the hope of offering this type of character training to many young people, Hahn introduced the Moray Badge scheme. In some respects this was similar to the Reich Sport-Abzeichen of Germany, the fundamental difference being that the Moray scheme was offered at two levels, the lower of which could be attained by anyone showing sufficient diligence.

With the advent of the Second World War training of this type was recognized as important, and the Moray scheme was widened to embrace all education authorities under the new name of the County Badge scheme. The difficulties of adapting the scheme to a wide variety of environments, together with the reactionary views of educationalists, militated against its propagation, and it was not until after 1945 that the scheme was further modified under the patronage of the Duke of Edinburgh, and was widely adopted.

In 1940 Gordonstoun was evacuated to Plas Dinan, Merionethshire, and in spite of the failure of the County Badge scheme Hahn was determined to pursue his adventure training. There was felt to be a need to improve the morale of sailors who, during the war, were subject to severe hardships. Financial help from Lawrence Holt of the Blue Funnel shipping line made it possible for Hahn to open the first of the Outward Bound schools at Aberdovey in 1941. The courses lasted for one month, and even in this short time he recognized that it was possible to direct the interests and thoughts of young people into fresh channels. The shortness of the courses meant that they were strenuous and had a controlled element of danger. The work of Gordonstoun and the Outward Bound prompted Arnold Brown to say that it was 'difficult to steer a good course between the rocks of compulsion on the one hand and the shifting sands of casualness on the other'. Gordonstoun under Hahn steered close to the rocks, facing dangers of all kinds with eyes open. This type of course was further developed by F. R. G. Chew and Arnold Brown in the Scottish mountains at Glen Feshie and Poolewe.

After the war the Outward Bound Trust enabled the movement to continue, and in 1950, following the example of Brathay Hall (opened in the Lake District in 1947), the Trust opened the first of the Outward Bound mountain schools at Eskdale. The movement flourished with new schools opening at Moray (1952), Ullswater (1955) and a school for girls in Devon (1959). The girls moved to the new centre at Rhownier (1963). The first of the foreign schools was set up by Hahn soon after the war. He was distressed by the moral collapse of the German people, and in particular of the young Germans. After trial courses, and with the help of the American and British Foundation for European Education, the first German school was opened in 1952 at Schlosswissenhaus on the Baltic. The second school was opened at Baad on the Austrian border in 1956 and a third has now been proposed at Berchtesgaden. Schools have also been opened in Austria, Holland, Malaya, Kenya, Nigeria and Australia. The Army has been impressed by this work and has opened its own schools at Aberdovey and in Norway. In the United States five civilian schools have recently been opened, but their methods of training and their fundamental philosophy are in many ways so dissimilar to the original aims that Lester Davies, warden of Ullswater Outward Bound School, suggested the term 'Outward Bound' should not be applied.

By the middle 1950s, therefore, the principle of character training through exposure to an unfamiliar and hostile environment had gained a wide acceptance. Various education acts in Britain had created and continued to promote a climate of opinion which made it possible for these innovations to be copied and adapted in the public sector of British education.

The dichotomy in British physical education which persisted into the present century was slowly subjected to pressures which made changes inevitable. In 1919 a new syllabus of physical training which was acceptable to both boys and girls was suggested, following the advice of Sir George Newman. This was superseded in 1927 by the *Supplement for Older Girls* and the *Reference Book of Gymnastic Training for Boys*. An immediate response to the new syllabus was the establishment at Sheffield of a college of physical education for men; the college closed in 1924 because of a shortage of suitable candidates. By 1933 the increasing demand for qualified men justified the opening of Carnegie College in 1935 and of Loughborough and Goldsmiths Colleges in 1937. The general relaxation of formalized physical education is illustrated by the provisions of the Physical Training and Recreation Act of 1937 and by the Social and Physical Training Grant Regulations of 1939. The Act emphasized the need for the provision of camps and training facilities for outdoor activities.

'The Ministry of Education may, in accordance with arrangements approved by the Treasury, make grants towards expenses of local voluntary organizations in providing, whether as a part of wider activities or not, or in aiding the provision of facilities for physical training and recreation, including, but not without prejudice to the generality of the foregoing words, the provision and equipment of gymnasiums, playing fields, swimming baths, bathing places, holiday camps and camping sites and other buildings and premises for physical training and recreation.

'A local authority may acquire, lay out, provide with suitable buildings and otherwise equip and maintain lands whether situated within or without their area, for the purpose of gymnasiums, playing fields, holiday camps or camping sites or for the purpose of centres for the use of clubs, societies or organizations having athletic, social or educational objects and may manage those lands and buildings themselves, either with or without charge for the use thereof, at a nominal or other rent to any person, club, society or organization for the use of any of the purposes aforesaid.'

The Act met with some scepticism and misapprehension since it coincided with the rearmament programme, but the foundations of the Act had been so long prepared that these fears, although convenient for the opponents of the Act, could not in all conscience be countenanced.

The Social and Physical Training Grant of 1939 made it possible for the Ministry of Education to make grants for the provision and maintenance of facilities for social and physical training, including the payment of salaries, the equipping of premises and for the incidental expenses of administration. The intervention of the war prevented the implementation of the Act and in some respects altered the emphasis in physical education towards tests of endurance. *The Curriculum and Examinations in Secondary Schools*, written in 1943, reflects the general climate of urgency:

'The experience of the war has shown that the young people of this country can respond to situations demanding courage and endurance; these qualities, we should hope, will be directed during school days to activities which give them scope and which lead to occupations making the same demands in the circumstances of peace.'

The influence of the newly established Outward Bound school can clearly be seen in this paper on curriculum:

'The raising of personal performance, won through the surmounting of individual difficulties by discipline and endurance, is of profound moral significance as well as physical. Individual effort to surpass one's own achievement, no less than co-operation and team work, is altogether to be encouraged. Among such standards we should certainly welcome carefully devised tests of endurance, of resourcefulness and enterprise suggested by the nature of the surrounding countryside.

'In this connection we would make mention of scouting and guiding, school camps, tours and sailing clubs which for many boys and girls provide, whether in term time or during the holidays, an incentive and a means to training in resourcefulness, self-reliance and ideals of usefulness and independence. Beside scouting other "courses" and "schools" and "movements" have been brought to our notice; their aim is to bring boys and girls in touch with the sea and mountains and in open-air tasks and ventures to build the moral strength and create the physical endurance which come from such contact.'

These recommendations were implemented in the 1944 Education Act, and local education authorities were able to interpret these provisions for recreation as they saw fit in their own areas. The Act made it the duty of every authority 'to secure provision for their area of adequate facilities for leisure time occupations in such organized cultural training and recreative activities as are suited to their requirements for any person willing to profit by the facilities provided for that purpose'.

Under Section 53(1) it was

'also the duty of every authority to secure that the facilities for primary, secondary and further education provided for their area include adequate facilities for recreation and social and physical training, and for that purpose a LEA with the approval of the minister may establish, maintain and manage or assist the establishment, maintenance and management of camps, holiday classes, playing fields, play centres and other places, and may organize games, expeditions and other activities'.

Participation in physical education at school was made compulsory under Part 1, Section 1(1) of the Act, and adequate facilities for the supervision of recreation by qualified teachers were prescribed. The sections of the Act concerned with recreation were further reinforced in *National Schools—their Plan and Purpose*, which pointed out that

'a period of residence in a school camp or other boarding school in the country would contribute substantially to the health and width of outlook of any child from a town school, especially if the care of livestock,

48

the growing of crops, the study of the countryside and the pursuit of other outdoor activities formed the bulk of the educational provision and were handled by specially qualified staff'.

At the end of the war it was not generally possible for LEAs to adopt the recommendation of the Act; financial stringencies required that efforts should be directed towards the expansion and modernization of the existing schools. As soon as the economic situation improved attention was directed towards the implementation of the 1937 Act. Derbyshire was the first authority to open a residential school offering opportunities for open country pursuits. White Hall Centre, near Buxton, was opened in 1950, and was largely due to the determination and inspiration of Sir J. Longland, the Director of Education. Longland was well known as a mountaineer, having been on the 1933 Everest expedition; he was also on the Board of the Outward Bound Trust and had close connections with Abbotsholme School. White Hall was therefore able to draw on the experience of most of the innovators in the field. For many years White Hall remained an interesting experiment, but it was not until the late 1950s, when its role had become fully established as an integral part of Derbyshire's education plan, that other authorities appreciated its potential and embarked on similar projects.

It was not only the education authorities but also the Central Council for Physical Recreation which fully grasped the importance of these early experiments. The CCPR, originally founded in 1937, was an organization serving the interests of the two hundred sports bodies which make up the Council. It offered help to sports bodies, to individuals and to local education authorities, and arranged courses for leaders and coaches. The CCPR became irrevocably committed to mountain activities when they established first a mountain training centre at Plas-y-Brenin in 1956 and the Scottish Council, founded in 1959, built Britain's only purpose built mountain training centre, Glenmore Lodge, in the same year. At both of these centres considerable emphasis is laid on the training of the trainers. Recognition of the importance of these centres was afforded in 1968 by the renaming of Plas-y-Brenin as the National Mountaineering Training Centre. The CCPR, since 1972 the Sports Council, is involved in the whole range of outdoor activities, but mountaineering and sailing are the only two which are served by residential centres; the sailing centre at Cowes was opened in 1969.

During the 1960s three reports significantly accelerated the trend towards physical recreation as opposed to physical education and emphasized the importance of outdoor activities. The most recent was the Newsom Report, published in 1963, which considered the education of average and less than average pupils specifically between the ages of thirteen and sixteen. In considering the physical education requirements of this group it was suggested that there was a greater need for diversity on the grounds that 'conventional gymnastics and field games, valuable as they are for those with skill enough to perform them, are not a source of enjoyment or self-esteem for all pupils'.

The report goes on to commend the work of the outdoor centres and suggests that the activities by them,

'although challenging, do not necessarily require the highly co-ordinated, refined skill typical of many sports and games, and outdoor activities have a special value for pupils with whom we are concerned. . . . These out of school activities would have the advantage of introducing pupils to recreational interests which can readily be carried forward into adult life'.

The Albemarle Report, published in 1960, was concerned with the age groups from fourteen to twenty years. The report recommended that the development of outdoor activities could be encouraged, indeed should be encouraged, by providing better facilities and a properly organized coaching scheme. They further suggested that established clubs should run junior sections and that regional pools of equipment should be provided.

These sentiments were echoed by the Wolfenden Committee in 1960. Appointed by the CCPR the committee pursued an examination of the whole spectrum of sport, games and outdoor activities. On the specific subject of mountain activities they recognized that

'the mould of tradition is irretrievably broken. We can no longer look to the well-established clubs to guide the steps of all those who, trained or not, are determined to have a go at one or other outdoor pursuit. And there is difficulty and danger here. In most other sports beginners can at wish or at need teach themselves by simply trying and practising.

50

Coaching will probably help them to learn more quickly and to make fewer mistakes, but trial and error will not usually lead to disaster. But in many outdoor activities there is an element of danger. In fact this element of danger may be not only integral to the sport but part of the attraction to those who wish to pursue it. It is not that actual danger is enjoyed for its own sake; its presence usually means that the situation has got out of control. What is clear is that the means of mastering potential dangers is to be found only in technique and applied experience. Supervision in this type of activity demands a high ratio of instructors, and there is therefore considerable need for greater numbers of experienced volunteers.'

In developing some of the recommendations of the Albemarle Report the Wolfenden Committee drew up an idealized five-point plan for the establishment of national coaching organizations. This recommends:

1. A well-paid national coach.
2. A graded coaching scheme with renewal examinations.
3. Qualified coaches should be released occasionally from industry both for instructing and for further training.
4. There should be a governing body for each sport.
5. Universities and colleges should direct students into these voluntary channels.

That these recommendation have been followed, almost to the letter, by the governing bodies says much for the power of the report, and at the same time shows that the need for the provision was already recognized by the governing bodies themselves. Their most important and far-reaching provision, however, was the establishment of a National Sports Development Council to be the financial and negotiating body between the various ministries and the governing bodies of sport. The National Sports Council was founded in 1965 under Dennis Howell, minister with special responsibility for sport.

The conference on 'The Countryside in 1970' again brought the picture of outdoor activities into focus, and Sir Jack Longland stressed that there was 'an astonishing drift of the whole range of subjects which we call physical education towards outdoor pursuits, towards mountains and moors and rivers, lakes and the sea'.

Just as the Wolfenden Committee had pointed out the dangers in these activities so Lord Hunt emphasized them in the Countryside Report by saying that:

'Apart from general education in primary and secondary schools, to make future adults aware of their mutual heritage it was also necessary to provide training in the actual skills and the know-how required for the safe use of the facilities, and for the development of more awareness of the danger of accidents inherent in adventure in wild country and on inland water. The work done by recognized centres in this field is very great but not great enough. Above all we need to develop higher standards of competence among the adults who organize adventurous activities among young people and more such organizers. The Mountain Leadership Training Board was established to undertake this work for mountaineering generally. The use of leisure was still not highly enough regarded as a subject of education. Outdoor activities should have a larger share in the curriculum of teacher training colleges and schools.'

Together these reports have influenced authorities in making provision for the recreation of the growing numbers who showed a greater interest in outdoor activities rather than in organized games and the old physical education. The growth of outdoor pursuit centres is shown in Fig. 2. The numbers are by no means exhaustive, but since many of the smaller centres are somewhat ephemeral in character we have included only those centres which are large and well established. This does not in any way mean that the smaller centres which may not have a permanent or resident staff do not serve a valuable purpose. The actual provision which is made by education authorities is not legislated and the facilities vary from mountain bothies completely devoid of any artificial comforts, such as the Edinburgh City's 'barn' in Glencoe, to the opposite extreme of a Scottish baronial castle near Dunoon, also run by Edinburgh. Between these extremes are the rural schools such as that at Cromdale which was converted to an outdoor pursuits centre by the Nairn and Moray Education Committee. The graph shows a relatively stable situation during the early experimental period where centres in the private and public sector of education were more or less numerically equal. It was not until the 1960s that the numbers increased rapidly with an increased rate of growth in the public sector.

The role of British industry in the promotion of outdoor pursuits lies mainly in their support of the Outward Bound schools.

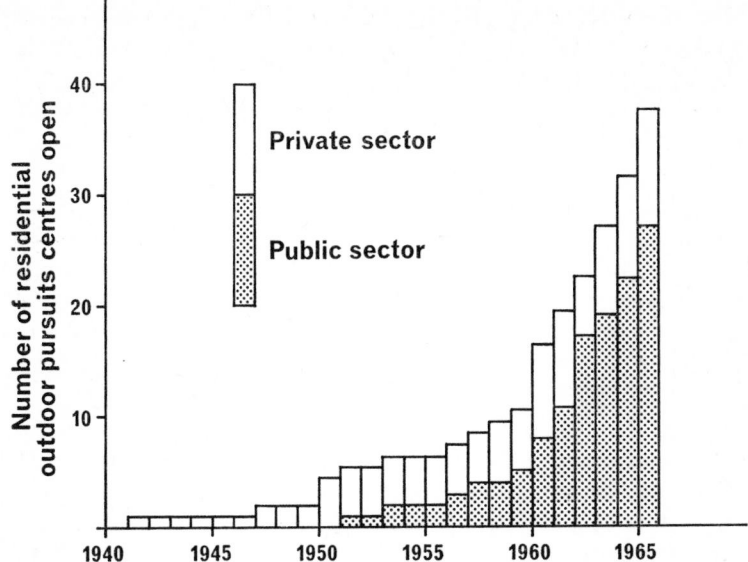

Figure 2   The growth of residential outdoor pursuits centres in Britain. (Only those centres with permanent staff and which are open throughout the year are included.)

The majority of students attending the Outward Bound courses are from industry. The main reason for this is that these courses are normally only available to students of eighteen or over, and students who are either still at school or who have just gone to a university are so heavily committed academically and have so many other demands on their leisure time that they are not generally available. Arnold Brown pointed out in 1962 that five hundred industrial firms regularly supported the courses and a further five hundred did so less regularly. Most industrial organizations who feel that this type of training is desirable are prepared to use the existing schools. Exceptions are found in the Plas centre run by Tube Investments in North Wales, and on a smaller scale the centre run in the Peak District by Park Gate Iron and Steel Company.

SUMMARY OF THE GROWTH OF OUTDOOR ACTIVITIES

Throughout the history of physical education changes have been in response to the prevailing social needs; changing circumstances have made new demands, the challenge of which has more often been taken up experimentally in the private sector of education. The success of such ventures was reinforced by legislation and subsequently became an integral part of the state educational system. The rigours and demands of war gave rise to physical drill which existed widely throughout Europe until the beginning of the twentieth century. The congested living conditions brought about by the Industrial Revolution made attention to public health through physical fitness a pressing need. A more humane attitude gradually replaced military drill and gave rise to a more liberal interpretation as illustrated by the adoption of Swedish gymnastics and the widespread introduction of organized games. These same trends are reflected in the replacement of the phrase 'physical training' by 'physical education'. Increasing opportunities for leisure and a more mobile society with greater affluence enabled an increasing sector of the population, particularly the younger element, to take an interest in the outdoor pursuits which, during the nineteenth century, had been the exclusive preserve of the moneyed classes. This interest is now being harnessed as an educational force. It remains to examine the growth of interest in the outdoor pursuits during the period which has been discussed. It is only by reference to these trends that it is possible to make coherent predictions about future demands, and to make sensible suggestions for the more intelligent use of this medium for education.

THE INCREASING POPULARITY OF OUTDOOR PURSUITS

By definition the outdoor activities have many elements in common, and it is not therefore surprising to find that their historical development has been very similar. The original motives for participation frequently lay in the search for encyclopaedic knowledge or as a fundamental means of transport in difficult terrain. These motives were gradually replaced by purely recreational aspects. The opportunities to indulge in these activities often demand both considerable leisure time and some expense. The early followers of these activities, therefore, came from the moneyed classes of the nineteenth century, who were the only groups who had both the means and the urge to satisfy their aspirations. As increasing numbers were freed from the drudgery of ceaseless toil so legislation was introduced to encourage their participation, and a climate of opinion arose which admitted that recreation was a valuable medium of remedial therapeutics. In all the outdoor pursuits there was, without exception in Britain, a slow but inexorable increase in popularity until the Second World War. This was followed by a phase of very rapid expansion, the course of which must be sought not only in an increase in leisure time opportunity, but also in a sociological change which permitted groups from all classes to take part in activities which had until this time been the exclusive preserve of the middle and upper classes. The rate of growth of these sports has continued to accelerate, and there is little indication that saturation level has yet been approached. In determining the total numbers involved in any of the sports innumerable problems occur. It is necessary to define the sport accurately and unambiguously; it is certainly not adequate to group, for example, hill walkers, mountaineers and rock climbers together. Having defined the sport it is necessary to decide the minimum commitment which could reasonably be expected of a participant. In some fields ownership of equipment may be a useful indication, but as a general rule we would expect a participant to be involved in his chosen activity on at least six days a year and further that he should devote part of his annual holiday to the pursuit. The sources of information which have made it possible to demonstrate the growing rate of interest and the total number of participants are very varied and are based on surveys whose parameters vary considerably. The reliability of the results was checked against other external parameters, and the indications are that they are sufficiently accurate to be of value. The results shown for Britain reflect trends in other European countries; minor variations can usually be explained in terms of differing environments.

Skiing is without doubt the most popular numerically of the outdoor adventure pursuits. This is as true of Britain as of any other West European country, a fact which is amply illustrated in chapter five. The growth rate of the sport in Britain is difficult to assess since the records of the National Ski Federation of Great Britain, which was only founded in 1964, are in fact incomplete. In 1968 there were eighty-five clubs affiliated to the NSFGB and its total membership was some 55 000. Major General Sir Ian

Graham estimated that in May 1968 there were still some thirty clubs who were not affiliated. The total membership of the NSFGB might well therefore have been about 70 000. It has been found in other sports and in other countries that only about one-third of the participants of any of the outdoor activities are affiliated to clubs and national organizations. This factor, if applied to the skiing population, would provide a total of over 200 000 skiers in Britain in 1968. This is a figure which is in accordance with estimates of the NSFGB. The very rapid growth in the sport, illustrated in Fig. 3a, is due to several important factors. The contribution of the tour operators and travel agents in promoting continental ski holidays cannot be overstressed. It is estimated that some 80 000 British skiers go abroad each year. The significance of the developments in Britain itself should not be overlooked. Although the most significant developments have occurred in Scotland during the 1960s, other areas have made some progress in the exploitation of natural facilities. The most important innovations have occurred at Aviemore in the Cairngorms where a multi-million pound commercial complex, consisting of hotels and recreational facilities, serves the needs of the rapidly expanding ski trade. Although significant, the contribution of the Scottish ski fields should not be over-emphasized. Based on the sale of tickets it was estimated that some 4 000 skiers used the ski areas on a perfect Easter Monday in 1968. In practice Scottish skiing is so subject to the vagaries of the north British climate, and is such a great distance from the main population centres in Britain, that its effect is, if not parochial, at least felt most significantly in the northern regions.

There is a strong correlation between degree of participation and interest and the proximity of the facilities. This is well illustrated by the popularity of skiing in some European countries shown in and discussed further in chapter five. In the case of Britain some various attempts have been made to overcome this particular problem by introducing artificial plastic ski slopes. The experience of the Edinburgh Education Committee, who were largely responsible for promoting this type of skiing in Britain, has shown that interest can be readily engendered and maintained. The success of their proselytizing has resulted in many other authorities taking an active interest in the provision of artificial slopes.

Sailing is the second most popular of the outdoor pursuits, and shows a rate of growth very similar to that of skiing (Fig. 3a). The period of explosive growth occurred in the period after the Second World War, and in particular since the 1960s onwards. The increase of sailing in British schools has had a profound effect on popularity. The demands are now such that public water undertakings have been asked to give serious consideration to the possibility of making provision for recreation, even at the risk of having to install more elaborate filtration equipment.

Canoeing, the second most popular of the water outdoor sports, has demonstrated the explosive development already observed (Fig. 3b). Technological advances have made it possible to introduce improved equipment, which has in turn meant that schools can afford to maintain fleets of robust canoes. Working in fibre glass is now included in the craft curriculum in a number of schools and colleges of education and in many of the mountain activity centres. By far the largest following is in the sphere of canoe touring where the network of canals in Britain provides excellent opportunities. The competitive element is less well developed, but both slalom and racing canoeing have shown significant increases since 1960.

The popularity of mountain activities in Britain is paradoxically large. The same trends in development can be seen as have already been noted (Fig. 3b). It is tempting to invoke the work of the mountain centres to explain this growth but, as will be discussed more fully later, their contribution, although significant, cannot alone explain the facts. As in other activities the growth is a manifestation of the climate of popular opinion which has in turn been moulded by legislation. The far larger and less well-defined groups of mountaineers and hill walkers are less easy to analyse. Reports from national recreation surveys and from national parks suggest that there are probably ten times as many walkers as climbers; this provides a current estimate of about half a million who visit the mountain areas of Britain and seek their recreation there by walking. At the other extreme are the climbers who visit the Alps and other mountain areas each summer, and who may spend some time climbing in winter in Britain. Estimates based on the use of alpine huts and alpine rescue statistics indicate that in 1968 about 2 000 British climbers visited the Alps. Inevitably the degree of commitment will vary in any sport, but this figure, 5 per cent of highly motivated and committed participants, is a proportion which has been observed in other activities.

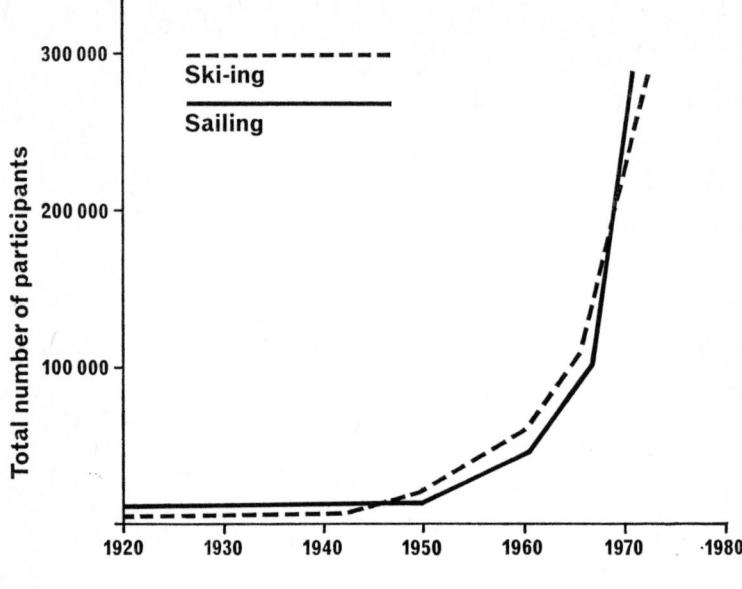

Figure 3a

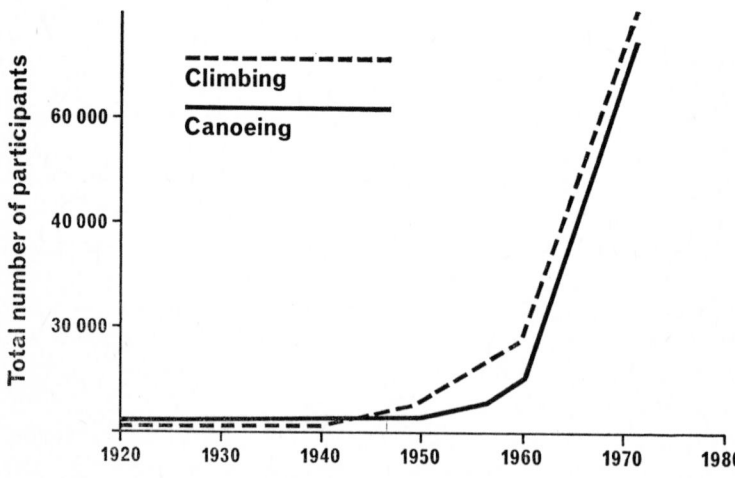

Figure 3b

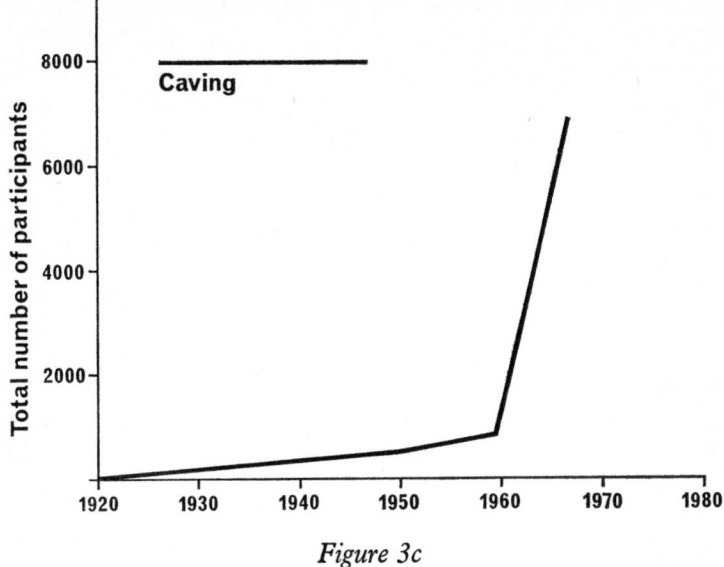

Figure 3c

There are two principal educational factors which have contributed to this rate of growth. The emphasis which has been placed on general mountaineering and expedition work by the physical education programmes in schools and youth clubs has helped to introduce young people to the mountain environment. The second factor is the necessary involvement in expeditionary work required in the syllabus and assessment of Duke of Edinburgh Award candidates.

In areas where natural facilities are lacking, artificial climbing walls have helped to provide opportunities for a basic introduction to rock climbing techniques. The publicity which has been given to climbing, not only in the press but also on television, has helped to capture the imagination of the public—a public only too ready to enjoy their sport vicariously but who seem to have responded to the demands of mountaineering with increasing enthusiasm.

Caving is very much of a minority sport among a minority group of activities. This is not peculiar to Britain; throughout Europe, even including such countries as France and Spain which are well endowed with karstic formations, the number of participants is small. As early as 1681 the Derbyshire poet, Charles Cotton,

59

believed that he had lowered nearly a mile of rope into Eldon Hole without it touching the bottom, and that a goose thrown into the hole reappeared at Peak Cavern with its feathers scorched by its passage through the infernal regions. The sport did not develop in Britain until widespread publicity was given to the descent of Gaping Ghyll by Martel in 1895. There is evidence to suggest that the first full descent was made almost fifty years earlier by Metcalf, Thomas and Henry Clapham, and William Elliot, together with a local farmer, who made their descent on 1st August 1846. The publicity given to Martel's achievement did not have the same catalytic affect as did Whymper's ascent of the Matterhorn. The increase in popularity of the sport has been slow so that even now there are only an estimated six thousand participants in Britain. In the history of other sports it seems that when the numbers involved reach this figure there is need for some form of central co-ordinating group. The caving clubs, which until recently have been organized on a parochial and regional basis, have now established a national caving association. Although a minority group there was a significant awakening of interest in the 1960s (Fig. 3c). The accidents of geology mean that opportunities for caving in Britain are limited. Regulations governing safety and training issued by the British Association of Caving Instructors are only just beginning to be agreed and adopted. Adverse publicity is afforded to caving accidents, and until such time as educationalists can familiarize themselves with these problems, and the sport is given the same measure of enthusiastic support as the other outdoor pursuits, it is difficult to see how it can normally be included in an outdoor education curriculum. The lack of popularity is further reflected in the absence of interest shown by students of physical education in ten colleges of education; without exception the students indicated that caving was of no interest to them.

The indication of growth in each of the activities considered shows clearly that the enthusiasm with which many schools and colleges have adopted these activities, either as complementary or alternative to traditional forms of physical education and games, is not in any way misplaced. The historical developments of environmental studies and outdoor pursuits have been examined in isolation. We have done this deliberately in the hope that by so doing it will be easier to appreciate the problems and potential when considering them together as outdoor education. It is obvious that both have many elements in common, and it is equally clear that some aspects of one reinforce the other, and it is now necessary to examine the provisions made to satisfy the requirements of outdoor education.

Chapter Two

BIBLIOGRAPHY

ALEXANDER T. *The New Education in the German Republic.* William Northgate, 1930.

ASCHAM R. *The Schoolmaster.* G. Bell & Sons, 1934.

BEAZLEY E. *The Countryside on View.* Constable, 1972.

BIRCH A. E. *The Story of the Boys Brigade.* Frederick Maller, 1959.

BOWKER E. *The German Youth Movement and its influence on education.* M.Ed. Liverpool, 1955.

BROWN A. *The Unfolding Character.* Routledge & Kegan Paul, 1962.

CARPENTER P. *The Outward Bound Schools; a means for the development and assessment of character.* Ph. D. Oxford, 1958.

COBURN O. *The Youth Hostel Story.* National Council of Social Services, 1950.

DAVIES L. Report on the Outward Bound Schools of America by the Outward Bound Trust (unpublished).

HENRY A. E. Some influences on the early developments of physical education in England. *Journal of Physical Education,* Nov. 1968.

JONES I. *An analysis of mountain accidents in North Wales.* Report of the BMC Mountain Safety Conference, 1972.

MCINTOSH D. *Landmarks in the History of Physical Education.* Routledge & Kegan Paul, 1957.

MCNAIR D. *The Development of Physical Education in Scotland before 1914.* M.Ed. Manchester, 1962.

MELDRUM K. I. *Mountain Activity Instructors' Certification.* M.Phil. Nottingham, 1970.

MELDRUM K. I. & ROYLE B. *Artificial Climbing Walls.* Pelhams, 1970.

NAWROCZYNSKI B. The demand for recreational and social education. *World Yearbook of Education.* Evans, 1965.

OGILVIE V. *The English Public Schools.* Batsford, 1957.

WADDINGTON M. H. *The developments in physical education in the schools of Wales.* M.Ed. Wales, 1951.

WARDLE D. *The Work of the Nottingham School Board.* M.Ed. Nottingham, 1961.

ZIEMER G. *Education for Death.* Constable, 1942.

Career Aspirations of Instructors in Mountain Centres. *Outdoors* 3, Jan. 1972.

Town and Country Planning Act. HMSO, 1947.

The Wolfenden Report on Sport. CCPR, 1960.

The Countryside Act. HMSO, 1968.

Recreation News 1–39, Countryside Commission (1969–72).

Recreation News Supplement 1–6, Countryside Commission (1970–1972).

Forestry Commission's Annual Report 1970–71.

Facilities for outdoor education

It is intended in this chapter to look at the three main areas of provision for outdoor education, in the schools, the specialist centres and the agencies involved in strengthening and supporting the development of facilities. We have chosen to illustrate the range of facilities, the varying programmes and the numbers taking part by the use of graphs, maps, example programmes and statistics rather than descriptive writing and explanation. As it is our belief that the most important contribution to outdoor education can be made by the schools we should look at this area first.

THE SCHOOLS

In a paper submitted by the National Rural and Environmental Studies Association to a conference held at Leicester University it was stated that

'the environmental approach to teaching was quickly adopted by primary schools, and in 1964 rather more than 25 per cent of the primary schools in England made their approaches to learning through environmental studies. The Association actively encouraged this approach to its members and, together with more recent work in this field by the Nuffield Primary Science Project and the Schools Councils Projects, the number of primary schools carrying out environmental studies must be more than 75 per cent.'

There is no doubt that there is an ever increasing demand from the primary school sector for more facilities, more money, more support for projects in the countryside sometimes solely study based, sometimes activity based—especially camping, youth hostelling, pony trekking, hill walking—and often a mixture of both.

In Scotland the Camp Schools Association runs five camps, and an authority like Edinburgh sends approximately 2 000 primary children per year in order to provide an opportunity for extension to the work being done in and around the city's schools.

In the main, outdoor education in the secondary schools cannot be quantified, in any case both the quality and quantity of the work being done vary so greatly that any statistics would be meaningless.

Outdoor education projects in the secondary sector rely heavily for their existence on the rather fortuitous presence of interested staff, and then the willingness of head teachers to support requests for time, transport, additional staff, equipment and money; and it is sad to report that often projects survive in spite of the lack of, rather than because of, a great deal of knowledge and commitment. We have devoted a separate part of this chapter to dealing with these problems. However, even without support many school teachers run exciting programmes, often out of school hours, but more are managing to break into the almost inviolate timetable.

Two extracts from school programmes give an idea of what is possible given support and a structure. The following list is taken from the programme of Braehead School, Fife.

Braehead School

Summer and autumn expedition programme

15–18 April	Canoeing	Firth of Forth
7–14 May	Girls' Highland Visit	Mull, Oban, Ben Nevis
16–18 May	Climbing	Western Highlands
20 May	Day expedition	Three Munros
21–28 May	Canoe—climbing	Loch Ericht, Ben Alder
30 May–3 June	Expedition	North West Scotland
6–15 June	Expedition	Knoydart
20–29 June	Expedition	Ross and Sutherland
3 July	Day expedition	Munros

4–16 July	Climb the remaining	Munros
20 July–24 Aug.	Expedition	Alps
1–8 Sept.	Highland Tour	Highlands
12–24 Sept.	Expedition	Wales and Ireland
27–29 Sept.	Expedition	Mull
6–10 Oct.	Canoe trip	Tweed
17–23 Oct.	Use of the school bothy	Rannich
29 Oct.–6 Nov.	Climbing	Cairngorms
17–23 Nov.	Youth Hostelling	Glen Nevis

It is interesting that this programme takes place during term time, and that the groups are made up from volunteers after the events are published throughout the school. No particular age range or form is timetabled for outdoor education. The George Pindar School, Scarborough, is fortunate in that it has a head teacher who is fully aware of the potential of the countryside as a relevant teaching area, and the following is taken from a report in 1972 on the school's activities:

'Outdoor skills in camping, walking, surveying, canoeing and sailing are developed through gradual training, and through these confidence grows. For example, first-year pupils when staying at the school's centre for a week take part in walks for five to ten miles, second-year pupils ten to fifteen miles and third-year pupils fifteen to twenty miles, planned by themselves. A similar progression of skills can be seen in the compass and map work so that, in the third year, pupils should be able to navigate by compass at night. Progression can also be seen in the environment used for the outdoor experiences. All years in the school use the school centre at some stage during the year; first-year pupils spend every night of their visit in the centre while third-year pupils have more nights under canvas.'

'Other environments used in the first year include a stay at an LEA centre to carry out field studies in biology, geography, history; in the second year potholing and hill-climbing activities are the basis of the programme which, along with advanced campcrafts, extends into late autumn.'

'The third year is known to the school as Adventure Year when pupils take part in week-end camps for small groups, in places chosen by the groups. These groups are not permanently supervised by staff but are subject to "lightning visits" at any time. Because the pupils have to look after themselves so much during the Adventure Year there is great emphasis on safety training and survival techniques. Other third-year adventure activities include participation in a long-established walk open to anyone and certificated if successfully completed; canoeing; sea sailing; attendance at guest houses. All culminate in the overnight sleeping-out exercise, the peak of the adventure activity and aimed at establishing very close, permanent relationships between staff and pupils who have shared the significant experience of spending the night outside, protected only by a sleeping bag in a polythene bag laid on the heather, after having walked twenty miles during the day. A cup of cocoa for supper, awakening at dawn for coffee, then breakfast at the school's centre. The rest of this adventure week is spent at the centre taking part in night hikes as well as a variety of day-time activities, including independent land surveying. The cost of the week is £1.50; the LEA pay expenses of the less well-off pupils. Equipment is made in school by the domestic science and handicraft departments or bought out of the school allowance. In the fourth and fifth years the school begins to concentrate more on examination work but not to the exclusion of adventure and outdoor activities. Art, geography and history groups use the school's centre for local study projects; non-examination pupils carry out a social service programme, helping to maintain and improve the centre. All have an opportunity of adventure activities farther afield: in Scotland, walking the Pennine Way or taking part in work camps in forestry districts.'

Like Braehead School and the George Pindar School, more and more secondary schools are introducing programmes which are deemed important integral parts of the school programme itself. Schools have been buying their own vehicles and their own centres and collecting adequate supplies of equipment and clothing so that exciting progressions can be built into the work for some time; and whereas formerly the annual camp or expedition might have been the sole contribution to outdoor education, now much more is becoming possible.

The provision of an outdoor centre by an education authority was often the only offering made, and though this was an extremely important gesture several authorities have seen the necessity of supporting both the school and specialist centre programmes with additional facilities and provisions. Fig. 4 illustrates the pattern of

Figure 4 DEVELOPMENT OF OUTDOOR EDUCATION IN WOLVERHAMPTON SCHOOLS

(30 secondary, 101 primary, 4 special schools)

2 teacher advisers appointed in 1968 to operate from a Teachers' Centre
↓
Duke of Edinburgh Award, Outward Bound and advanced expeditions
Development of field studies, outdoor pursuits and allied activities
↓
Equipment purchased from capitation/school fund

PLUS a 50% grant from the LEA for equipment
↓
School journey allocation

IN-SERVICE COURSES (Wolverhampton L E A)

1966
Canoeing—Canoe building
Outdoor pursuits (N. Wales)
Skin diving—Geography

1967
Canoeing—Canoe building
Field studies (Towers,
  Llangollen)
MLC (Towers)—Geography
  Sailing
Canoe building (Bingley St)

1968
Canoeing (N. Wales)
Canoe building—Geography,
  Campcraft, Environmental
  studies (Ryton)
First aid
MLC (Towers)
Sailing (Himley)

1969
Canoeing (N. Wales)
Canoe building (Eastfield)
Integrated studies (Towers)
Skiing. Winter mountaineering
MLC (N. Wales)
Sailing (Bala)

1970
Canoeing (Ironbridge)
Orienteering (Beaudesert)
MLC (Towers)
Sailing (Bala)
Skiing (Towers)
Dry skiing (Dudley)
Lightweight camping
  (Beaudesert)
Mountaineering

Unless stated to the contrary courses occurred in LEA centres

CENTRES (Wolverhampton L E A)

Place	When opened	Time used
Residential		
Ryton (Canvas Camp)	1958	April/July
Pwllheli (Farmhouse and Hutments, Field Centre)	1959	Feb./November
The Towers (N. Wales Outdoor Education Centre)	1959	All year round
Beaudesert (Canvas)	1967	April/July
Llangollen (YHA)	1967	April/July
Staunton on Wye (YHA)	1968	May/October
Malvern (YHA)	1968	May/July
Duntisbourne (YHA)	1969	May/July
Day Resources Centres		
Bala (Sailing)	1968	June/July
Pensnett (Sailing)	1966/68	May/July
Chelmarsh (Sailing)	1967	June/July
Himley (Sailing)	1968/70	April/October
Gailey (Sailing)	1970/71	April/October
Bingley St School (Boat and Canoe building)	1966/68	All year round
Eastfield School (Boat and Canoe building)	1968/71	All year round
Dunstall Park (Canoe base)	1971	All year round
Ironbridge (Canoe base)	1971	All year round

SCHOOL ASSOCIATIONS

Aston St (Teachers' Centre) has a large room which has been made available as a display area and to keep information concerned with L E A Schemes
Canoeing—Sailing—Orienteering—Mountaineering

Environmental Studies
All Associations are involved in Developmental Work

development made possible by Wolverhampton LEA, whilst Fig. 5 shows the structure of provision for outdoor education in Edinburgh Corporation's Education Department, and the following account describes briefly the work within that structure:

Edinburgh embarked upon this provision for outdoor education in a similar way to many other education authorities, and by earmarking something in the order of 1 per cent of the total educational budgets was able to develop the following schemes. Benmore, Centre for Outdoor Pursuits, was opened six years ago. In many ways the centre was responsible for an increase in the awareness of the potential of outdoor pursuits, mountain crafts and water activities; and because it was capable of taking fifty pupils each week and was provided with excellent staff and equipment the impact was to be found not only in a new attitude but also numerically. Benmore is in Argyll National Forest Park, and as such has access to a remote mountain area and fine lochs and rivers. Clearly the centre was not satisfied with introducing young people to this fine situation in a very professional manner without there being some continuity between their work and that of schools. Two specific ways of achieving this proved successful. The centre's staff visited city schools and, of even more value, teachers were encouraged to accompany their pupils to the centre and to attend 'in-service' training courses at the centre, so that they could be knowledgeable about Benmore's work and the pursuits themselves.

Gradually the centre has become able to gauge the likely demands of schools and plan accordingly whilst schools have come to make more appropriate use of the centre.

Many outdoor centres have to face the problems of inadequate communication, and whilst it would be naïve to suggest that the two methods mentioned provide an automatically successful technique for avoiding these, they are worth pursuing along with other methods.

Lagganlia Centre for Outdoor Education is sited in the Cairngorms and has been open for four years. The centre, and the ski lodge adjacent to it, are capable of housing thirty people.

Lagganlia is Edinburgh's second specialist residential centre and is quite deliberately different from Benmore. It is intended that it should be used principally as an extension to school or club activities. Leaders are expected to provide their own course pro-

Figure 5 PROVISIONS MADE BY THE EDINBURGH EDUCATION COMMITTEE FOR OUTDOOR EDUCATION IN SCHOOLS

Special provision	Main participants	Events
Adviser in Outdoor Education Assistant Adviser	School associations (sailing, canoeing, orienteering, skiing)	courses expeditions
Benmore Centre for Outdoor Pursuits	camp schools (primary pupils)	staff training
City Centre for Outdoor Pursuits	school and college programmes	race training
Sailing Base Pony Trekking Centre Lagangarbh Barn	teachers' courses	
Hillend Ski Centre	youth and community and independent clubs	
Lagganlia Centre for Outdoor Education		

gramme and be able to instruct within that programme. Equipment, transport and guidance from the warden encourage the production of sound, safe work in an area which contains a mountain range of over 1 000 metres and the rivers Spey and Findhorn. Outdoor pursuits include mountain crafts in winter and summer, orienteering, canoeing and skiing and, as the centre is very close to Nature Conservancy ground, to deer forest, to alpine plant growing areas, to nature trails and a variety of historical and geographical features, teachers take the opportunity of interesting their pupils in the total environment as part of a designed course, or as a complete course in itself. The two residential centres are dissimilar but complementary. Both rely heavily on the work being done in the city and this takes two main forms. Hillend Ski Centre and the City Outdoor Pursuits Centre provide the specialist facilities in Edinburgh and, of course, the other major area of work is in the schools. The instructors at Hillend teach nine hundred school children to ski every week of the school year on the largest artificial ski slope in Europe. There is provision on the centre's timetable for school ski clubs, for practice for schools going abroad to ski, for race training, and for the hire of equipment for short trips to Scottish snow ski areas.

Pupils trained at Hillend are a force to be reckoned with in skiing events in Scotland, and it is indicative of the value of this sort of provision that, for example, most of the ski racing team are only thirteen years old, that a considerable number have been already for extra training to the Alps and that two of them are now training with the British team.

The City Centre is an experimental and information base, an instructional area, a source of equipment, transport and instructor supply, and a meeting place for teachers, pupils, courses and clubs. There are, in the centre, a pool for canoeing and sub-aqua climbing walls, a fibre-glass workshop, craft room, lecture and club rooms and equipment stores but, in the main, activities radiate from the centre rather than remain within it. Attached to the work of this centre is the City Sailing Base and the Pony Trekking Centre.

The development and use of these four specialist centres are carefully planned and interlocked so that a very large proportion of the requirements of schools can be met, and also that the demands of new schemes can be provided for even at short notice.

It is encouraging to be able to record a considerable growth of activity in schools led by able teachers. This enthusiasm and ability have been of significance not only in the use of the centres, but in the emergence of exciting school programmes which are completely self-contained. More and more schools are purchasing vehicles, buying equipment, involving more and more staff, and producing continuous, progressive outdoor projects.

Outdoor education is in evidence in primary, special and secondary schools, colleges, camp schools and the youth service. Courses at the primary camp schools contain experiences in orienteering, camp craft, youth hostelling and countryside knowledge, and these are extended in the city and then into the secondary schools. Some of the secondary schools provide general programmes of work on the environmental side, others on outdoor pursuits and, yet others, a mixture of both, in school time and out of it. Some schools concentrate on one activity only. Certainly it would be very difficult for a considerable number of teachers and pupils to define a 'school day' or a 'school holiday'. The expressions hardly exist in any recognizable form for them.

This situation has not arisen purely by chance. The Education Department, four years ago, embarked upon an extensive inservice training programme for teachers, and now well over five hundred teachers have attended courses which have ranged from the general, e.g. outdoor education, to the specific, e.g. mountain leadership.

Whilst the main aim of the department is to introduce a large number and wide variety of youngsters to activity and study in the countryside, there is an obligation to those who have become interested and to those who are both enthusiastic and able. The numerical breakdown of these numbers is shown in Fig. 6.

The combination of Hillend and Lagganlia can, it has been seen, cater not only for the development of hundreds of young average skiers but for the training of top-class performers. Appropriate use of Benmore by school orienteering clubs, for example, will have a similar effect, especially as this activity is organized by a schools' association too. Orienteering provides a good example of the rapid development of a new pursuit encouraged through the agencies of a residential centre and a specialist school association. Seventeen secondary schools, nine primary schools and 173 individuals

73

Figure 6 ANALYSIS OF PARTICIPATION IN OUTDOOR
EDUCATION FROM EDINBURGH EDUCATION
DEPARTMENT. (*Figures in brackets indicate total
number of pupils at school and total number of schools*)

STAFF

Number of instructors	25	
Number of temporary instructors	20	
Number of associated staff involved heavily in activities run in conjunction with the department	16	
Number of teachers attending courses 1969–1970	366	
Number of teachers attending Benmore and Lagganlia with courses 1970	81	

SCHOOL WORK 1970–1

Total number of pupils at specialist centres 1969–70	10,000	(65,000)
Number of secondary schools with comprehensive programmes	17	(23)
Number of school camps	10	
Number of schools skiing (in Scotland)	12	
Number of schools skiing (abroad)	8	
Number of schools attending pony trekking centre (primary and secondary)	23	
Number of secondary schools in Sailing Association	10	
Number of schools in Orienteering Association (primary and secondary)	26	
Number of schools in Skiing Association	20	
Number of secondary schools in Canoeing Association	10	

SPECIALIST WORK 1971

Number of pupils in ski race training group	40	
Number of pupils on major expeditions	65	
Number of secondary schools represented on expeditions	13	(23)
Number of pupils in clubs for advanced work	60	

belong to the Edinburgh Schools Orienteering Association. In 1970 the association organized six events in which there were 452 competitors, twenty-eight of whom gained their advanced badge. A considerable number of these competitors went on to compete in local and national events, and one Edinburgh school orienteer was selected for the British team. The Edinburgh Schools Sailing and Skiing Associations and the Edinburgh Schools Canoeing Association can each produce equally impressive records, i.e. eighty-two competitors in the first canoe event of the year and the establishment of a Schools Sailing Base in the city.

Certainly it is expected that those young people who are involved in the extensive training and execution of advanced expeditions or competitive work in Turkey, the Alps, Poland, Austria, Switzerland, Iceland and Norway will provide a nucleus of extremely able and enthusiastic young people well able to organize their own activities, which is one of the department's objectives.

Of course some schools can cater for themselves entirely and do not need to pass their youngsters on to associations or specialist centres or to join centrally organized expeditions. It is the belief of the department that it should make as much sensible provision as possible but not pressurize everyone to use it or to use it in one particular way. With this in mind the department is now making provision for another category of young person, the one who prefers to join a club and become involved in the development of an activity programme organized by the members themselves.

Having provided the means for young people to take part in hazardous pursuits any responsible education authority must recognize its obligation to provide some form of controlled continuing opportunities. Adult clubs are often reluctant, for a variety of reasons, to accept the responsibility for the further training of young people. It is often necessary to overcome this traditional and unfortunate attitude by establishing, as Edinburgh have had to do in some cases, independent clubs to bridge the gap between leaving school and joining an adult club.

Northumberland is an authority which has concentrated a great deal of its efforts into providing residential bases to serve developing school programmes. These centres, all in the country, form the following impressive provision:

Centre	Accommodation	Staff
Ford Castle	36	Warden + 2
Howtel	28	Warden + 1
Wauchope	42	Warden + 2
Kielder	28	Warden + 1
Newton	16	Warden + 2
Catton	28	Warden + 1
Sunderhope	10	Unmanned
Allenheads	28	Warden + 1
Carrshields	28	Warden + 1

Perhaps the most significant recent development is the increase in the number of authorities that are providing city or county bases readily accessible to teaching staff, and containing all the items and expertise required by them to expand their school programmes. It is this sort of development which we now need to look at in more detail.

OUTDOOR EDUCATION IN THE NON-RESIDENTIAL SITUATION

It is well to remember that teaching in the outdoors may not be intrinsically more valuable than that undertaken in the classroom. There are indeed some decided disadvantages in developing a programme of outdoor education when the staff/pupil ratios are taken into account and the likelihood of a disproportionate amount of time, in blocks, has to be considered and, especially, if it is designed to contribute only towards filling the extra year caused by the raising of the school-leaving age. The Scottish Education Department's Circular 804 on outdoor education states:

'If Outdoor Education is to make a proper contribution to the general education of pupils a structured programme of work in it must be developed to ensure that during their school careers pupils have a continuous and progressive outdoor experience as an integral part of their whole educational experience, including if possible at least one period of residence at an outdoor centre.'

Unfortunately the circular does not go on to say how this could be achieved, and what support might be forthcoming to produce the necessary staff, facilities and other resources.

First of all some of the implications of such a policy. It is necessary to make it clear that areas chosen for outdoor pursuits will normally be safe and not subject to dramatic changes of weather or contain serious difficulties; but as skills develop, and more resources are provided, especially for outdoor pursuits, there will be a natural progression into areas and activities where the possibility of risk is increased. At all times the leader of any party engaging in outdoor education must be certain that each member of the group is:

1. Sufficiently skilled and experienced to cope with all foreseeable situations.
2. Of an appropriate age and maturity for the selected activity, and that medical evidence is obtained declaring an individual to be fit and healthy enough to participate safely, and that
3. Parents are made aware of the nature of pursuits and give their approval to these being undertaken.
4. Any insurance arrangements by or for the leaders, group members and controlling authority are fully understood.

The controlling authority must accept responsibility for the pattern and development of outdoor education, but once in the field the leader is responsible for the safety and well-being of his group and must be free to make appropriate decisions.

So a great deal of responsibility is being placed on teachers who usually have no point of contact or reference to a head teacher or senior member of staff once an exploit away from the school is embarked upon. No distinction can be made between what is conducted in school time or out of school hours, yet often head teachers are unaware of what is being undertaken and have little experience themselves of the nature of the activity. The same sort of responsibility is not regularly given to a teacher in the classroom so it is as well to examine what is required.

The techniques of leadership are complex, and yet provide the most critical factor in both the conduct and development of outdoor education with young people. Although such skills as group management and technical competence can be improved considerably through experience and training, many leadership qualities are innate. Before leading young people in potentially dangerous activities these essential qualities of leadership must be confirmed by others with more experience and proven ability.

The qualifications available at the moment through the Mountain Leadership Boards, Canoe Unions and National Schools Sailing Association, for example, commendable though they are, cannot, in our opinion, be considered as adequate substitutes to full-term training in a college of education, nor are they automatic guarantees of someone's competence to make accurate judgments about young people's abilities, or correct decisions in times of stress. At this point in time it is only possible for us to put forward a number of constructive suggestions for the development of outdoor education in schools, bearing in mind the major recommendations of both the Scottish Education Department and the National Association for Outdoor Education, and the requirements of changing educational patterns exemplified by the raising of the school leaving age.

Whilst taking into account the fact that aspects of outdoor education are, and should remain, in existence in both the primary school and the first year of secondary school, the second year of secondary seems the most suitable time to be used as a major introduction and the base to a progressive programme of outdoor education for all pupils. This is the time when an increasing number of demands are being made by teachers to extend educational programmes, and it is inevitable that there will be the need for considerable adjustment to many existing timetables if they are to be met. However, this is the time, in our opinion, to make a properly designed beginning to outdoor education for all pupils. At this age the theme should be one of 'exploration and inquiry' in all the aspects of outdoor education. In outdoor pursuits activities such as camping, coast and hill walks, pony trekking and orienteering are the most suitable. These pursuits, coupled with camps and youth hostel visits, general studies and observation in the countryside, would serve several purposes:

1. The encouragement of exploration and inquiry.
2. An introduction to a range of safe experiences.
3. A protection from the development of specific skills at too early an age.
4. A sound base for later progressive activity, and an increase in the range of pursuits to include canoeing, sailing, skiing, rock

climbing, and of more specific studies or interests, and longer periods in residential type situations.

This system does, of course, presuppose that there will be opportunities and provision available for all pupils who wish to extend their experiences in the third, fourth, fifth and sixth years based on the present systems of 'minority time', 'choice of activity' and 'clubs' designed to fit the requirements and availability of examination and non-examination pupils. It would be as well now to look at some of the practical requirements and areas for examination.

Timetabling

Two main timetabling methods emerge as possibilities:

1. *Block timetabling* whereby everyone in several consecutive sessions experienced an aspect of outdoor education and then began another block for a different aspect and so on for one year. This would require the production of mini-syllabuses in outdoor education and the working through them on a rotational basis.

2. *Day release* where on a selected number of prearranged days per year pupils would be released from their normal timetable to experience the range of activity within outdoor education, again using mini-syllabuses.

It should be considered desirable to include in any timetabling a one week residential course using youth hostels, camps and specialist centres in addition to the more constant exposure through either of the methods outlined.

The difficulties of timetabling are not to be minimized, but they can be overcome. One serious problem, largely out of everyone's control, is that of seasonal differences which limit the range of suitable activities, particularly in the winter when weather and daylight prove limiting factors. However, imaginative programming and the provision of appropriate resources can to a certain extent overcome even this problem.

Organization

The emergence of an assistant headmaster (leisure), as suggested in the Scottish Education Department memorandum, *The Structure of Promoted Posts in Secondary Schools*, in the school organization may be important, as it is expected that a person appointed to that position might be given responsibility for the development and coordination of outdoor education. It is only unfortunate that the emphasis on 'leisure' has been decided upon.

The organization at the teaching level could be achieved in two ways:

1. The formation of a department organized in the normal way.
2. The creation of a 'project team' as representative of all those teachers involved in outdoor education which would produce and 'feed in' an organized, linked programme.

Whichever method might be adopted there is the necessity of having a trained, able teacher as project leader or head of department, and for arrangements to be made for the release of appropriate teachers from their own subject departments in order that they could contribute to the development of either separate or linked aspects of outdoor education.

Staffing

The problem of staffing is one not easily overcome at the moment, and yet any development is seen to hinge on the provisions of enough able teachers. Consideration needs to be given at national and local level to the following ways of counteracting the problem:

1. The training of semi-specialist teachers in a diploma year.
2. The contribution to be made by specialist instructors.
3. Student assistance.
4. A central pool of replacement staff which would fill the places of those teachers working out of school.
5. Auxiliary staff to drive, look after equipment, prepare facilities, etc.
6. A greater degree of support to be given to those teachers utilizing considerable quantities of their own time in the development of outdoor education.

It is encouraging to hear of optimistic forecasts of the pupil/teacher ratio being lowered to cater for the extra demands of small group work activity which is likely to be increased with the raising of the school leaving age.

Facilities

In order to achieve the sort of situation envisaged by Circular 804 there will need to be a considerable extension of resources. A school will need to increase its supplies of equipment, finance and transport, and will probably require an equipment store room, drying room, a garage/boat store and an area for lectures, meetings, displays and projects. The education department will need to consider the desirability of providing day resource centres in or near to a city or county, staffed, equipped and full of information and material, and both large and small residential centres in appropriate places.

Significant increases in finance, transport and equipment will be inevitable, and these aspects of development should be looked at in three ways:

1. Education department initial provision and grant aid.
2. School maintained, based and provided out of per capita allowance.
3. Central pool provision.

A system based on the requirements outlined is, of course, quite different to the classical way of providing for outdoor education, which has previously been limited to the purchase of residential centres, usually about one hundred miles from the base authority. Despite the value of visits to such centres, and the vast amount of effort and dedication put in by members of their staff, this method, as the only provision, has proved somewhat unsatisfactory to the pupils. It has often served to isolate the centre from the main stream of education, making communication difficult and therefore effectiveness somewhat less than ideal; it creates a confusion in objectives, and often provides only an isolated experience of activity for young people and a short-term acquaintance for staff. This is discussed in greater detail in the next section. An offshoot of this system has been the purchase by schools of their own 'centres', but here again the implications are manifold, especially if the education department will take no responsibility for the centre or make provision for its use. It is fundamental that the basic grounding should be provided by the schools and that centralized resources should be provided and serve, support and lead, when necessary, the development of outdoor education in the schools. It will have become increasingly obvious that there is a great deal to be researched, thought out, planned, programmed and provided for if outdoor education is to continue to be encouraged in schools as an accepted part of every child's education. The anticipated large-scale increase of activity in the countryside, thought to be one way of making an extra year demanding and attractive, is in our opinion one which deserves considerable attention rather than tacit acceptance if it is to be conducted in isolation from other school subjects and without a progressive element.

There is the possibility that this will become another area for 'dabbling in' or 'testing', and that pupils will receive unconnected experiences on the grounds that a wide variety of activity is automatically valuable. Young people may well be led into situations by enthusiastic but untrained teachers which could prove both damaging and disastrous. The numerical impact alone on the countryside and places of particular interest or beauty is of considerable importance and an implication which should not be neglected.

Those teachers, well experienced, knowledgeable and responsibly taking young people into the countryside, know of the values of directing energies, interests and enthusiasms towards worthwhile experiences. It is this knowledge, combined with the awareness that a structured approach is becoming even more essential, which should form the base for new and safe developments in outdoor education which, given the right guidance, leadership and resources, can provide for opportunities through an initial basic introduction and lead to many new, differing experiences, fields of exploration and relationships which may not be available to all pupils through other methods of education.

OUTDOOR EDUCATION IN RESIDENTIAL CENTRES

A list of outdoor centres (Appendix A) is poor recognition of both the pioneering role and the extensive influence of such a specialist group. Many centres spread their expertise through primary and secondary school children, youth club members, school teachers and youth leaders, colleges of education, further education and university department students. Centres like Bewerley Park

(Yorkshire) and Whitehough (Lancashire) take over one hundred pupils at a time, but most centres have accommodation for between thirty and fifty students. The distribution of centres (Fig. 7) illustrates dramatically the concentration in the Lake District and North Wales of the outdoor pursuits centres, and they are often a hundred miles from their authority, whereas the authority field study centres are often close at hand.

This siting of residential centres has occurred on an *ad hoc* basis; as old properties have become available in suitable environments they have been acquired and adapted by education authorities, very often without a sufficiently careful survey of the available resources, and without due regard to the aims of the centre and the needs of the students. The siting of the centre will clearly be a factor in determining its pattern of use. Centres situated at a considerable distance from the schools that they serve can only be economically used for extended visits. For example, it would not be realistic for a comprehensive school in London to use a residential centre in Argyllshire for weekend visits; such a centre could be used extensively during the vacations and during the term time for week-long visits. A centre such as Whitehall, run by the Derbyshire LEA and situated at Buxton, is no farther than fifty miles from the most distant school within the authority. Local schools could reasonably use the facilities on a day to day basis, whereas even the most remote schools could be expected to make short visits over weekends. The actual site selected should provide an opportunity to work in a wide variety of environments and habitats to which there should be readily available access. Although situated on the edge of the Peak District National Park, Whitehall Centre does not have access to the hills immediately dominating the centre. Ideally when they leave the centre for an expedition students should experience a feeling of freedom rather than one of constraint. The centre should combine accessibility for its clientèle with an element of remoteness, a compromise which it is not always easy to achieve, but without which many of the opportunities for social integration may be lost. The environment should possess considerable variety, and intensive use of any one area should be avoided in the interests of conservation. A varied environment also provides opportunities for the centre's staff to maintain their enthusiasm. The building itself will in many cases be an adapted large country house and its matured aspect,

83

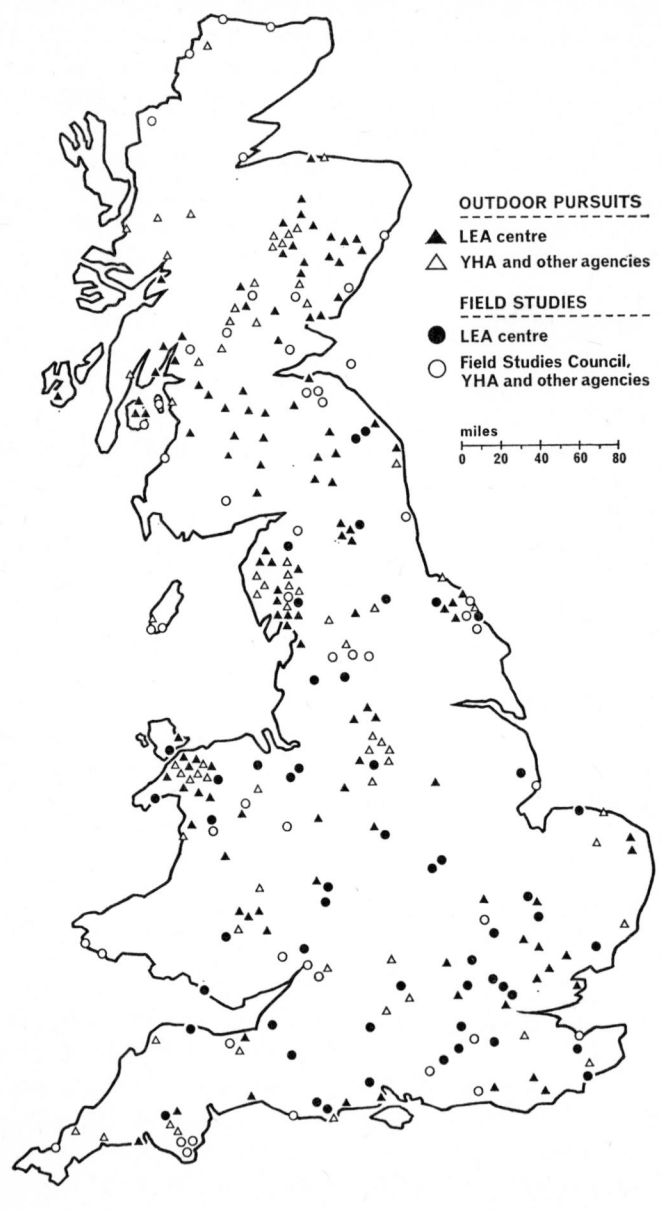

OUTDOOR PURSUITS

▲ LEA centre
△ YHA and other agencies

FIELD STUDIES

● LEA centre
○ Field Studies Council,
   YHA and other agencies

miles
0   20   40   60   80

although not necessarily an architectural masterpiece, will almost certainly blend with the countryside in such a way that no offence is given. This is not always the case in a new building, although both Glenmore Lodge and Lagganlia Centres in the Cairngorms have used natural wood, which in spite of modern designs weathers rapidly to blend sympathetically with the surroundings. The problems of car parking have been discussed in many other places, but strategic use of existing woodland can provide adequate screening.

The buildings themselves, whether old or new, or whether specifically planned for outdoor pursuits or for field studies, should provide the following accommodation:

Reception Areas. One of these should be sited prominently at the front of the building and should provide all the information which the normal visitor can be expected to require. This area should be quite distinct from the area where students will return from expeditions and excursions. This latter area should include:

1. An initial changing area where all outer garments are removed.
2. An adjacent drying room which gives access to:
3. Shower rooms for boys and girls, together with toilet facilities.
4. There should also be a laundry area with either tumbler dryers or separate small drying rooms.

Figure 7   *The distribution of residential outdoor centres in Britain.*

> *Note : The addresses of the centres are to be found in the following :*
>
> 1. *Outdoor Studies Centre in Scotland. A report by the Committee on Education and the Countryside, available from The Scottish Education Department, St Andrew's House, Edinburgh.*
>
> 2. *Directory of Centres, Council for Environment, 1970. Available from the Department of Education and Science, Elizabeth House, York Road, London SE1 7PH.*

Student Sleeping Accommodation. This should be in the form of small cabins holding not more than six students. The cabins should be arranged in such a way that various ratios of boys and girls can be accommodated with propriety. The rooms might have tables and chairs for private study.

Staff Accommodation. This accommodation should be separate from the student wings and should consist of flats suitable for both single and married instructors. There should be rooms available for instructors, guests and for visiting staff. The principal at least should be provided with a detached family house. There should be a bed-sitting-room in the students' wing for a duty instructor.

Sick Bay. There should be a small sick bay where students can be isolated, both for their own comfort and for the protection of other students.

Work Areas. There should be work rooms fitted with apparatus appropriate to the type of work to be undertaken.

Library. The library should contain both technical reference books and a selection of general reading. Tables and chairs should be available.

Games Area. The games area might be incorporated in a general recreation area where there could also be facilities for discothèques and for serving drinks.

Shop. The shop should satisfy the day to day needs of the residents, and might at the same time sell essential equipment which it might be difficult to replace immediately and which is not available on loan or hire to the visitors.

Stores. The equipment store must be quite adequate and should contain workshop areas and separate areas where equipment can be issued.

The exact arrangements of the facilities will depend on the resources available, but it is unlikely that adapted buildings will meet these requirements precisely.

That schools and centres should work together is axiomatic, but so often there is no such rapport. It has been said that the residential training centres are responsible for flooding the countryside with visitors. This is far from the truth. Examination of the facts in the field of mountain activities shows that agencies other than the residential centres have a greater impact on the increase of participants. Although there is no statistical evidence available for the other outdoor pursuits, it is probable that the same conditions apply. As a result of surveys which have been made, and from the personal observations of many of the wardens of mountain centres, it appears that few of the students who visit the local education authority centres are sufficiently convinced of the merits of the activities to want to pursue them as committing recreations. The case of the National Mountaineering and Sailing Centre is rather different; the |students visiting there are already highly motivated, either through their college course work or from their own choice. Choice is perhaps the key to the problem. Although many of the school children who visit centres do so from choice, this choice often lies between being at school or not being at school rather than from a genuine desire to participate in the activities. The reasons for school children visiting centres vary, depending on the policies of the schools, the centres and the local education authorities. In some cases it is simply a question of packing off the least able students who are not academically involved and whose presence in school is a perennial source of difficulty. The other extreme is the students who are carefully screened so that the image of the school will be upheld. Between these extremes lie all the other possibilities, but often a course is treated in isolation and there is seldom any preparation for it and even less often is there any feedback to examine the effects of the course. This brings into question the whole problem of the viability of residential outdoor pursuit centres. The centres are generally regarded as serving four aims:

1. Character training.
2. An introduction to lasting leisure-time pursuits.
3. An experience in community living.
4. Countryside appreciation.

If we take each of these facets of work in turn it will be seen that the viability of the concept of residential training of this sort can be severely criticized.

The most serious attempts to assess changes in personality as a result of exposure to hardships and the anxiety of a hostile and unfamiliar environment were undertaken by P. Carpenter in the case of boys and by Betty Strutt in the case of girls attending Outward Bound courses. There was little evidence to show that personality traits were initiated, but it did appear that some existing traits might be reinforced as a result of this experience; the traits which were emphasized, however, may not now be regarded as desirable in present society. Students became dissatisfied with menial tasks and developed an element of independence, aggression and self-assertion. These traits were not strongly developed, and further research may show that there is no significant change in personality. The Outward Bound courses are arduous and use the unfamiliar environments of mountains and sea as a testing medium rather than a facet of heritage to be admired and appreciated. The courses last for a month and it is therefore no surprise to find that the local education authority centres, whose courses normally last for only two weeks at the most, and whose principal aim is not to change or develop character, have an effect even less marked than the Outward Bound.

If we now move on to the second purpose which is given, namely the provision of a lasting and worthwhile recreation, we are faced with an even less satisfactory outcome. Less than 1 per cent of students introduced to mountaineering in local education authority centres take up the sport seriously. The rate of increase in participation has already been shown to be of the order of 2 000 a year. This does not allow for those who for one reason or another have given up; the real figure for new participants each year must therefore be more like three thousand, and the total number of students attending residential mountain training centres each year is of the order of thirty thousand; if the above figure of one per cent is applicable then all the new climbers are introduced through formal training in centres. This is clearly not the case—many are introduced by their schools directly or through friends or relations. The real figure for follow up in centres is therefore more likely to be less than half a per cent. In the case of a typical LEA centre taking a thousand students a year there will be only five who take up mountaineering. Applying elementary cost benefit analysis to this fact means that each climber costs the authority some £6 000. This is a great deal of money, particularly when it is appreciated that the climber has only received a basic introduction to the sport. It is a totally inadvisable expenditure if one further realizes that most mountaineers cease their activities during their mid twenties. Residential centres therefore cannot be regarded as viable if their principal aim is to provide young people with lasting leisure-time pursuits. In fact it would be difficult to find pursuits which were less suited to a lasting interest than rock climbing, canoeing and caving. Surveys have shown that other pursuits, such as sailing, camping, walking and skiing, are more susceptible to a lasting interest, and clearly family recreation such as golf, swimming, gardening or mountain walking are better suited to provide an extended recreation.

The opportunities which are afforded by a residential environment can provide an experience in community living, and as such is a viable and worthwhile social experience. We question whether it is necessary to provide centres whose staff are so highly qualified, and where the staffing ratio is so generous, if this is the main function of the centre. The experience of living in a community could be provided just as satisfactorily and at a very much lower cost in a youth hostel, or from camping.

The final purpose of residential outdoor pursuit centres is to offer an introduction to the appreciation of the countryside. This, we feel, could be the *raison d'être* of many centres, and whereas the other aspects of the work are valid it is on the success of providing an integrated course covering the varied aspects of countryside awareness that centres stand or fall. This will mean that centres may need to alter their basic courses and may mean the introduction of stronger environmental study elements. Hopefully there are signs that this course has already been adopted. The heyday of the mountain training centres was during the early 1960s, but there has been a noticeable reduction in the number of centres opened recently; there has, however, been a large increase in the number of field study centres opened.

A residential centre with its own staff does provide an introduction to outdoor pursuits, but only with previous knowledge of the students is it possible to react sympathetically to their particular interests and fears, and to select situations which are best calculated to achieve the desired reaction. Lack of knowledge can have its positive dangers; inevitably some students exhibit a marked degree of curiosity and aggression, and by the time these traits have been recognized a problem situation or accident may already have occurred. The teacher in school is in a very much better position to be aware of these difficulties, and has the opportunity to provide a carefully graduated and progressive programme. One is forced to ask whether a residential centre costing £35 000 a year, and introducing a thousand students to either field studies or outdoor activities, is a better proposition than twenty teachers doing the same technical work for about four times as many students. Perhaps the ideal is to provide both for peripatetic teachers within the schools and for a residential centre which is charged with the in-service training of teachers and with running courses of a more advanced type for students who show particular aptitude, and who have progressed beyond the stage which is appropriate to the school-based teacher. The centre could offer courses to those who for any reason were not able to make use of the peripatetic staff or who had lost their own staff responsible for these activities. The system adopted by Edinburgh Education Committee and explained in the previous chapter approaches the ideal most closely with two city based centres staffed by permanent and peripatetic staff and two residential centres. It is only a large authority which could attempt provision on this scale, but we feel strongly that the school-based provision is the more important.

The qualifications of the staff will vary enormously depending on the aims of the centres. In the outdoor pursuits centres there was a tendency some time ago to appoint experts well versed in the technical skills who may or may not have been good instructors or teachers. There is now a trend to appoint teachers who also have the necessary expertise. Most staff are expected to help in a wide range of activities; the scope of their versatility is illustrated by a survey of instructors' time in mountain centres (see Fig. 8).

The staff responsibilities are often clearly defined by sets of rules offering guidelines for the safe conduct of each of the activities. In spite of this much of the responsibility for making serious decisions still rests with the teachers in the field and because of the recognized dangers involved some education authorities have made special provisions for the insurance of staff.

The work undertaken in the field centres is of a very different nature, and obviously caters for the more academically orientated student. Courses at the Field Studies Council centres are often directed towards teachers, colleges and universities and to sixth-form students. The staff are not only highly qualified, but through

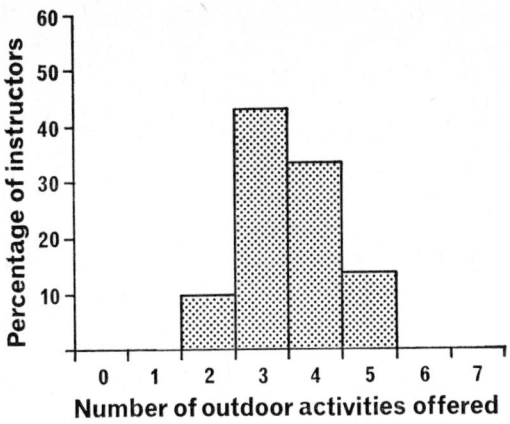

Figure 8   Number of activities offered by instructors in mountain centres.

their intimate knowledge of the neighbourhood are able to illustrate facets of the programme by the best examples in the area. They are also conversant with the special problems of conservation in their area, and can plan their courses in such a way as to protect these interests. Most of the field centres are equipped with lecturing and laboratory facilities. Inevitably the facilities available are somewhat limited, and in the case of much original research it is necessary to analyse the field data at great length in a more sophisticated laboratory. Physiological research into the effects of immersion in cold water, recently undertaken by the Department of Physiology at Edinburgh University's field centre, would have been valueless had they not been subject to examination by computer. The Field Studies Council is not the only agency to recognize the importance of providing facilities for practical field work. The Youth Hostels Association, for long a reactionary group satisfied with the pre-war concept of providing cheap accommodation for underprivileged young people, has adopted a progressive attitude towards field studies; several of their hostels are now equipped with field study laboratories, libraries, lecture and reading rooms. The need for this type of accommodation is likely to become greater as the whole subject of environmental studies and outdoor education is more widely accepted in schools, and particularly if it becomes recognized as a CSE and 'O' and 'A' level examination.

Figure 9 NUMBER OF PEOPLE USING THE OUTDOOR CENTRES DURING 1970

Figures obtained from the Field Studies Council

Summary of subjects	Dale Fort	The Drapers'	Flatford Mill	Juniper Hall	The Leonard Wills	Malham Tarn	Orielton	Preston Montford	Slapton Ley	Total
Biology	1 414	712	1 244	713	961	623	1 032	604	1 111	8 414
General and environmental studies	43	230	—	106	54	13	—	126	65	637
Geography and geology	412	870	80	782	797	994	775	753	469	5 932
Art and photography	106	21	215	12	19	19	—	19	40	451
Archaeology	23	—	—	—	—	—	—	159	31	213
Others	—	54	10	—	14	74	28	12	—	192
Totals	1 998	1 887	1 549	1 613	1 845	1 723	1 835	1 673	1 716	15 839

Categories of visitors	Dale Fort	The Drapers'	Flatford Mill	Juniper Hall	The Leonard Wills	Malham Tarn	Orielton	Preston Montford	Slapton Ley	Total
'A' level	1 533	1 006	925	1 494	1 501	1 178	1 395	1 123	1 126	11 281
Other forms	—	211	14	—	39	—	8	119	87	478
Colleges of education and teachers	112	292	184	57	127	249	246	115	292	1 674
Universities	211	193	78	15	97	164	143	104	95	1 100
Land-linked professions	46	49	2	2	—	34	—	4	24	161
Amateurs	96	136	346	45	81	98	43	208	92	1 145
Total	1 998	1 887	1 549	1 613	1 845	1 723	1 835	1 673	1 716	15 839

In any examination of the programmes of centres it is interesting to observe that the centres which contain a large element of outdoor pursuits also devote time, and often staff, to the promotion of an understanding of the countryside by the students, but that it is very rare for those centres established in the main for field studies to include any element of outdoor pursuits, even map and compass work. The statistics for use of the nine Field Studies Councils centres (Fig. 9) are of particular interest and relevance, and give alongside the full list of centres very definite indication of the total numbers of young people being involved in countryside work through the centres alone.

AGENCIES INVOLVED IN OUTDOOR EDUCATION

Appendix A gives a list of the agencies involved in education in the countryside. The British Wildlife Society's Junior Explorers section serves to illustrate the role of such independent groups. The society claims that in the five years since its inception members of the Explorers have travelled 48 300 miles, made 186 expeditions and visited thirty-eight islands off the coast of Britain. Both the Brathay Exploration Group and the British Schools Exploration Society are long established, the latter since 1932. On the inaugural expedition a group of eight visited Finnish Lapland; they were all from public schools, but now the organization copes with eighty each year, and the members come from all types of schools, industry, commerce, cadet forces and clubs. The Brathay Group was formed in 1947, and has of course a permanent base and close association with Brathay Hall and field study centres. The range and scope of expeditions for young people have gradually been extended until at the present time the annual programme of some nineteen expeditions at home and overseas includes visits to countries as diverse as Iceland, Greenland, Norway, Poland, Yugoslavia, Tunisia, Kenya and Uganda.

When all the facilities are put together it will be seen that there is a formidable array of provision available to help educate young people in the problems and potential of the countryside, and perhaps the lists serve to show how much more effective a voice there could be if the array became a cohesive group. We have outlined in a previous chapter the many philosophies behind outdoor educa-

Figure 10 FIGURES FROM THE DIGEST OF COUNTRYSIDE RECREATION STATISTICS

Figures obtained from the Countryside Commission

	1950	1960	1965	1968
Membership of county naturalists trusts	825	3 006	—	33 272
Estimated number of active naturalists	—	100 000	270 000	—
Royal Society for Protection of Birds				
Adults	6 500	14 200	—	35 500
Juniors	—	—	—	18 500
Membership of the National Trust	25 000	95 000	155 000	160 000
Membership of the Ramblers Association	4 600	11 300	13 771	17 193
Membership of the YHA	210 142	181 958	219 336	219 547
Membership of the British Spelaeological Association	—	120	177	185
Number of clubs affiliated to the British Mountaineering Council	36	92	135	152
Number of clubs affiliated to the Royal Yachting Association	714	1 011	1 332	1 491
Number of clubs affiliated to the British Canoe Union	12	124	256	357
Number of branches affiliated to the British Sub-Aqua Club	—	49	—	217

1970—Authors' Estimates

Campers	3 000 000
Canoeists	55 000
Mountaineers	800 000
Sailors	500 000
Skiers	350 000
Rock Climbers	40 000

tion, but as this chapter has been concerned with detailed practical evidence and statistics it is perhaps relevant to conclude with a table of figures from the *Digest of Countryside Recreation Statistics* (Countryside Commission, 1969), which provides us with the numbers of people involved in the pursuits nationally (Fig. 10).

Primary school children at the Hillend Ski Centre, Edinburgh

The development of skill, as well as physical endurance, can be as demanding in mountaineering as in other recreations

A primary school group

The lecture room and laboratory at Garth Hostel which specializes in field studies

Seashore ecology with secondary school children

The Cowes National Sailing Centre run by the Council of Physical Recreation

A study on boulders with primary school children

Benmore Outdoor Centre, one of the Edinburgh Education Committee's centres near Dunoon

BIBLIOGRAPHY

BEAZELEY E. *The Countryside on View*. Constable, 1972.

MELDRUM K. I. Career aspirations of Instructors in Mountain Centres. *Outdoors* 3, No. 1, 1972.

PARKER T. M. *An Approach to Outdoor Activities*. Pelhams, 1970.

Field Studies Council Annual Report, 1969–70.

Digest of Countryside Recreation Statistics. Countryside Commission, 1969.

Directory of Centres. Council for Environmental Education, 1970.

National Association for Outdoor Education. Circular—Safety in Outdoor Education, 1972.

National Rural and Environmental Studies Association. Conference Report, Leicester University, 1971.

Outdoor Education and Outdoor Centres. Circular 804, 1971, Scottish Education Department.

Outdoor Study Centres in Scotland (Committee on Education) in the Countryside, 1971.

The Structure of promoted posts in Secondary Schools in Scotland. HMSO, 1971.

Standing Consultative Council on Youth and Community Services. Scottish Education Department, 1966.

Training for outdoor education

The different approaches to the problems of providing for outdoor education are as varied as the agencies which are responsible for their implementation. From an examination of the available facilities made in the previous chapter, it is apparent that there are both elements in common and factors in divergence in the provisions made. These differences are, in many ways, the perennial and ubiquitous problems of education: teachers, schools, curricula and examinations.

In the field of outdoor activities many teachers have, and still do, devote many of their out of school hours to the introduction of young people to these activities, but this is often simply the enthusiasm of experienced amateurs, who have gained great pleasure from their own pursuits, wishing to pass on this enjoyment to others. Although enthusiastic many of the people who have voluntarily accepted responsibility for the safety of groups have too readily assumed that enthusiasm is a substitute for experience, and that experience alone is an adequate means of assuring the safety of a group of novices. Mountaineering, where the dangers are perhaps more apparent, serves as a good example to illustrate the historical development of legislation for qualification in outdoor pursuits.

QUALIFICATIONS

One of the first agencies to appreciate the potential demands for mountaineering was the British Mountaineering Council (BMC), which was founded in 1944. A survey conducted by them in 1944 showed that throughout Britain there were already sixteen mountaineers who were acting as mountain guides, and it was felt that it was 'desirable to register and possibly test all men who wish to practise as professional mountain or rock guides':

1. In recommending criteria for guides the BMC relied largely on the experience of the Swiss Alpine Clubs.
2. Although not particularly demanding, the scheme was criticized by Cecil Slingsby who advocated the introduction of of a lower level of certificate, the general standard of which would be the same as that for a rock climbing guide, but a knowledge of rope work would not be required. A high standard of route finding in mists and snow and a general knowledge of his own district being essential.
3. The scheme suggested by the BMC was criticized by the Association of Scottish Climbing Clubs (ASCC), who regarded the qualifications as, in some respects, less stringent than those required to obtain membership of some of the Scottish clubs.
4. In spite of objections the scheme was generally approved and was implemented in August 1946. Candidates were required to have at least two years' climbing experience, details of which had to be provided. The experienced had to include the following:

   (a) three long walks, one of which must be in winter;
   (b) twelve difficult rock climbs of grade II or V, according as to whether a certificate as a walking guide or a climbing guide was sought;
   (c) Some experience in winter conditions, including three expeditions;
   (d) for climbing in Scotland a knowledge of snow and ice climbing was essential.

Local committees of the BMC were charged with the administration of the scheme and, in the case of experienced climbers, could waive any test; if a test was conducted it should last for two days and had to cover all the normal facets of mountaineering in addition to rock climbing.

Of the original sixteen practising guides only five eventually registered, and the first certificate was issued on 21st January 1947. The scheme for guides certification is largely the same now as it was then, although in many respects the role of the guide has been superseded by that of the mountain instructor.

Early hopes that the BMC expressed in the new guides scheme, when they noted that 'some clubs were embarrassed by applications from young people wishing to be taught to climb', were largely misplaced. By 1960 the BMC had to reply to an inquiry covering the career of mountain guiding by saying that

'we do not think it would be advisable to recommend anyone to seek to become a guide either in this country or in Switzerland as a full-time career. So far as this country is concerned, we think that it is very much of a part-time occupation, or alternatively is run in conjunction with a guest house or something similar.'

Over the years the number of guides has increased to between thirty and forty, but the sentiment expressed by the BMC remained valid; the majority of these are employed as mountain instructors. It is perhaps important at this stage to distinguish between the two groups of professional mountaineers. Guides are principally concerned in taking a client up a route to provide both maximum safety and enjoyment for the client. The instructor on the other hand is expected to combine the role of guide with that of teacher, a point which will be elaborated later in this chapter.

The increased popularity of mountaineering resulted in an increase in the number of accidents. In 1960 several of the guides in Wales said that in view of the high rate of accidents in the mountains, and the proportion of young people involved, 'we feel that the whole system of guiding in this country needs to be taken more seriously. Men and women in charge of young people in the mountains should be required to hold a certificate and should not be allowed to lead a party in the mountains unless they have this requirement'.

Prompted by these words and conscious of the problem themselves the BMC, together with the Central Council for Physical Recreation, formed the Mountain Leadership Training Board in 1961. By 1967 the scheme of certification, which in many respects followed the 1946 recommendations of Slingsby, had achieved such success that the CCPR felt justified in writing that 'in regard to the supervision of journeys involving mountaineering and field

100

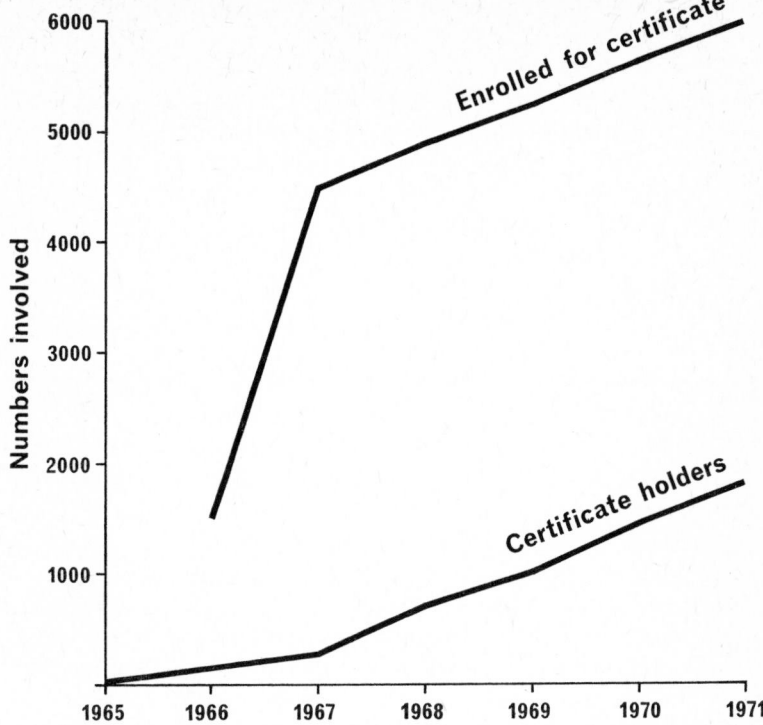

Figure 11   The development of the Mountain Leadership Certificate scheme.

studies and recreation courses in hills and mountains, leaders should be expected in future to hold the Mountain Leadership Certificate (MLC)'. Unfortunately there are still insufficient qualified teachers with the MLC for all education authorities to insist on these qualifications. Some twelve authorities had, by 1969, introduced various forms of legislation to determine the conduct of groups in the mountains. Some had gone the full way and insisted on the MLC, others required their teachers to have gained approval from some appointed expert within the authority, others had made no provision at all. The details of the syllabus and regulations for the MLC are given in Appendices B and C. The demands are time consuming, and although the numbers holding the MLC are increasing steadily (Fig. 11) it is unlikely that it will be possible for all authorities to make rigorous legislation for a number of years.

As in the case of the BMC's Guides' Certificate the Scottish mountaineers felt that there should be a separate certificate for winter in Scotland. The Scottish Mountain Leadership Training Board's regulations are given in Appendix C. By 1971 there were only forty candidates who held the winter certificate, and since this represents the accumulated total over seven years it was recently suggested that the standard should be slightly lowered. Not only is the certificate important in its own right but it will have increasing significance, since it forms an integral part of the Mountaineering Instructor's Certificate. The details of this scheme, which was first proposed by the Association of Wardens of Mountain Centres in 1964, are given in Appendix D.

The scheme is run at two levels, the lower level of the Mountaineering Instructor's Certificate and the higher Mountaineering Instructor's Advanced Certificate. The complete national scheme of mountaineering certification is shown in Fig. 12.

Although this is the only nationally accepted scheme of certification there are many parochial schemes designed to meet particular local requirements. These qualifications range from the Boy Scouts' Rock Climber's Badge to the Mountaineering Association's Tutors' Certificates; between the two are schemes like the Rock Climber's Leader's Certificate at Whitehall Centre in Derbyshire.

It is perhaps pertinent to examine the effect of introducing qualifications in the field of mountaineering in so far as it is reflected in accident statistics. Far from showing a dramatic decrease in the number of accidents there is apparently a slight increase in risk. It is, however, too early to show how effective such a scheme may be ultimately.

In the case of rock climbing it has been shown that the risk remains constant, whatever innovations in equipment and technique may be introduced. This fact suggests that climbers accept a certain minimum margin of safety and that any developments in the sport have more the effect of increasing the difficulty of climbs attempted than of reducing the risk; danger is an integral part of the sport and accidents play an inherent part.

Although the field of certification in mountaineering has been covered in some detail it should not be thought that this is a unique provision. In most of the other outdoor activities there is an equally

Figure 12   AGENCIES RESPONSIBLE FOR MOUNTAINEERING CERTIFICATION IN BRITAIN

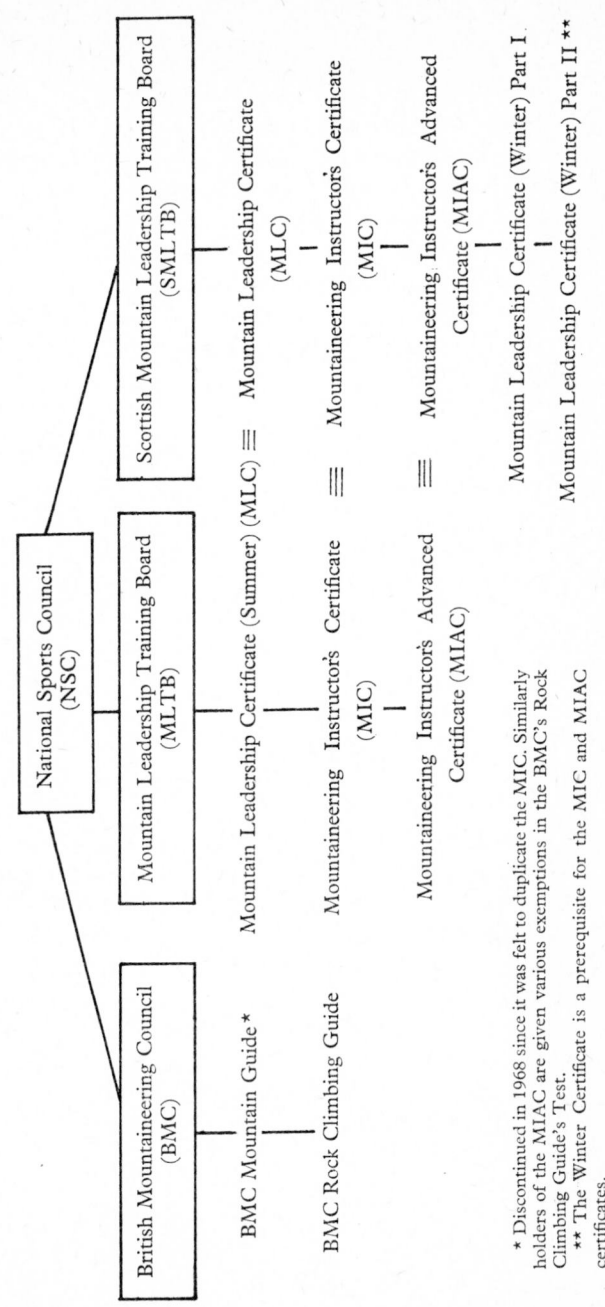

* Discontinued in 1968 since it was felt to duplicate the MIC. Similarly holders of the MIAC are given various exemptions in the BMC's Rock Climbing Guide's Test.
** The Winter Certificate is a prerequisite for the MIC and MIAC certificates.

rigid and hierarchical system. The recommendations of the Wolfenden Committee were quite explicit on the establishment of coaching schemes. Reporting in 1960 they advocated:

1. A well-paid national coach.
2. A graded coaching scheme with renewal examinations.
3. Qualified coaches should be released occasionally from their normal work to take part in instruction and to further their personal training.
4. There should be a governing body for each sport.
5. Universities and colleges should direct motivated students into the appropriate coaching schemes.

The British Canoe Union, founded in 1936, has followed the Wolfenden recommendation more exactly than some other governing bodies, and in some respects has improved on the original outline. There are two inter-related schemes; the series of personal proficiency qualifications is an essential part of the coaching scheme. The wide publicity and the obvious attractions of the scheme have had the effect of reducing the total number of accidents by almost half at a time when the number of active canoeists is increasing. The value of the scheme is without doubt and it is quite clear from an examination of the syllabus (Appendix F) that a minimal amount of information and training in technique has had very profound effects. The risk involved in canoeing is far greater than in mountain walking, and perhaps the dramatic reduction in the risk cannot be anticipated in the case of the hill walker. A further factor is that a number of the hill walking accidents are the result of coronary disease and other natural causes of death, and it may indeed be a pious hope to reduce the accident level below that which has already been achieved.

As in the case of the MLC, local education authorities have not been slow to grasp the opportunity for legislation. Many authorities now expect those involved in teaching canoeing to hold the Senior Instructor's Certificate. This is, however, a minimum qualification and only one measure of the competence of a teacher to instruct. The Senior Instructor's Certificate initiated in 1966 or the coaches' certificates are more appropriate qualifications for the task of group teaching.

Both mountaineering and canoeing are popular activities; caving on the other hand is a minority sport. The accident risk in caving is

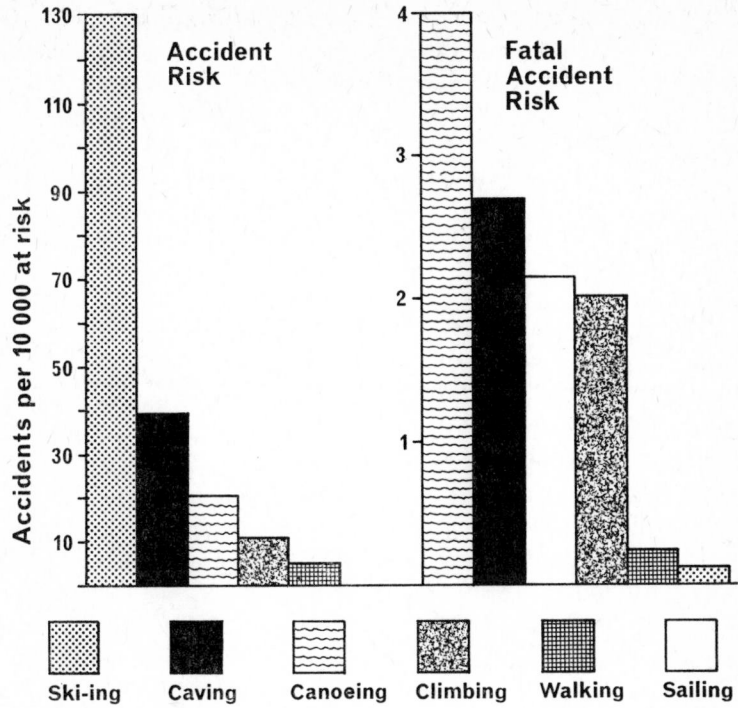

Figure 13   Accident risks in outdoor pursuits in Britain for 1970.

considerably greater than in the other outdoor pursuits (Fig. 13). Accident risks are as much as five times greater than the highest risks experienced amongst canoeists before the introduction of the BCU coaching scheme. Another fact which helps to put the risk in perspective is that in 1959, the year that Welsh climbing guides were concerned about the risk of accident to mountain walkers, the risk to cavers was fourteen times as great. It is not therefore surprising that education authorities have been reluctant to accept the responsibility for instructed caving, and will continue to exhibit caution until the whole sport can be regulated and more instructors can gain qualifications comparable in authority to those of the BCU and the MLTB.

From the survey of a minority pursuit, with its only recent centralization and provision for certification, the most significant contrast can be made by examining the provision for skiing. Not surprisingly Britain was not to the fore in the provision of professional qualifications. The first steps were taken on the Continent, where participation in the sport was greater and where the demands from the rapidly developing tourist industry applied direct pressures. The first tentative steps towards formal training were taken in Norway when the brothers Hemmestveit opened the first ski school in 1880. After experience in mountain warfare training the first ski instructors' training centre was opened at Mont Revard in France in 1933. The demand for trained instructors is proportional to the number of skiers requiring instruction. In Britain this demand was only established with the commercialization of skiing in Scotland. Unlike many of the other outdoor pursuits the need for training and qualifications is created not so much by a need to reduce the inherent dangers in the sport but more to provide a technical service. The accident risk in skiing is extremely high and the National Ski Coach estimated that the risk of minor injury is as high as one in two during a two-week ski holiday. The injuries are very seldom fatal, but are often serious. The risk involved is widely recognized and is generally accepted by individual skiers, education authorities, tour operators and insurance companies. Good equipment and good instruction can both help to reduce accidents, but they must remain a very real possibility. The first skiing tests in Britain were introduced by the Ski Club of Great Britain. These, like the system of étoiles in France, are a measure of personal competence, but in no way are the tests an indication of ability to teach. One exception to the rule is the First Class Touring Certificate, which requires its holders to be competent to lead groups of skiers on easy high alpine glacier tours and demands an elementary knowledge of rock and snow climbing. This is the only certificate which examines the alpine climbing ability of British mountaineers. Many continental ski schools protect their teachers by denying other nationalities, whether qualified or not, the right to instruct. It is not therefore surprising that few British skiers are interested in the touring qualification; in 1967 only one candidate gained the award.

In 1962 the British Association of Professional Ski Instructors (BAPSI) was founded. The standards of the certificates are comparable with ski instructors' certificates on the Continent. After the initial two certificates additional categories were introduced in 1965. Each of the grades is a necessary prerequisite for the examination for the next grade. Details of the various requirements for each grade are given in Appendix F. In 1966 the British Council of Ski Instructors was formed in an attempt to deal with the conflicting views in the training and grading of instructors and the standardization of ski schools. The unreliability of snow conditions elsewhere in Britain means that all the examinations until recently have been undertaken at Glenmore Lodge, the Scottish Sports Council centre at Aviemore. Demand for the courses, particularly at the lower levels, arises more from a desire to achieve recognition and status among the candidates rather than to gain a full professional qualification. Whereas some local education authorities and the Scottish Department of Education have provided grants for teachers taking the lower Ski Party Leader's Certificate, they have shown reluctance to provide similar support for the higher awards, which they regard as professional qualifications for which there is no immediate demand from schools. The total numbers involved are not great but they nevertheless satisfy the present demands in Scotland, particularly since the continental ski teachers who belong to the Association of Ski Schools of Great Britain (ASSGB) are also included.

By virtue of the professional character of the BASI qualifications, in spite of the fact that in 1968 the professional title was omitted, it is very difficult for amateur skiers to gain any recognized ski teaching certificate. To overcome the problem the National Ski Federation of Great Britain (NSFGB) started courses in 1968–9 for both elementary and advanced ski teachers. For teachers responsible for taking ski groups there is a very basic one-day course for ski party organizers. The important aspects of pre-ski training are covered by a special Pre-Ski Teacher's Certificate, and even in the esoteric field of artificial-slope skiing there is an Artificial Slope Instructor's Certificate. Perhaps because skiing is by far the most popular of the outdoor pursuits under discussion the administrative structure is more complex. Fig. 14 illustrates this complexity, together with its related scheme of certification.

The virtual monopoly of qualifications in Britain which was held by the British Ski Clubs until the 1960s is paralleled by the role played by the Royal Yacht Club in the certification of sailing. The highest award in sailing, the Yacht Master's Certificate, is issued by the Department of Trade and Industry (formerly the Board of Trade). The certificates devote considerable attention to naviga-

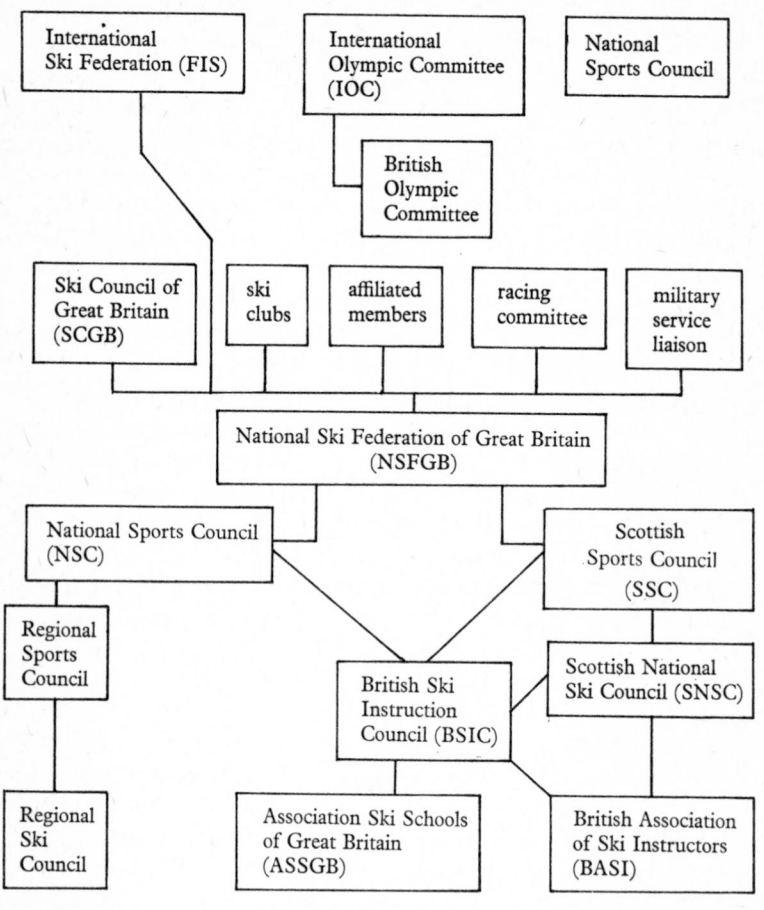

Figure 14 THE NATIONAL STRUCTURE OF SKIING IN BRITAIN

CERTIFICATES

	Amateur		*Professional*
BSIC	NSFGB: SNSC	BASI	instructor
	ski party leader		assistant instructor
	pre-ski instructor		ski teacher
	artificial slope instructor		

tion and interpretation of charts. The different aspects of coastal and ocean sailing are covered by the Yacht Master's Coastal Certificate and the Yacht Master's Ocean Certificate. The details of the syllabuses are given in Merchant Shipping Notice 534. It has been found that something between 150 and 200 hours is required to cover the syllabus and the work is assessed in a six-hour examination at the end of the course. At the moment some 209 people hold the ocean certificate and 265 hold the coastal certificate. Whereas the armed services require the highest grade of qualification for their advanced sailing instructors, education authorities and commercial ventures do not set their sights so high. The first of the sailing certificates was introduced by the Royal Yacht Club. As in many of the other spheres of outdoor pursuits the whole problem of certificates in sailing is under review. The RYA were primarily concerned with their own members and were anxious to improve standards of safety and sailing ability. The educational role was left more to the National School Sailing Association (NSSA). In 1972 the NSSA and the RYA jointly introduced an integrated system of certificates (Fig. 15). As in the field of canoeing, a certificate of personal proficiency, the RYA Advanced Certificate, is regarded as the minimum level of competence upon which a candidate can base his instruction. The initial instructor's certificate will equip a teacher to instruct the crew of a single dinghy at a time and under the direction of a more highly qualified teacher. The NSSA instructor will be expected to have additional knowledge relevant to his educational and safety responsibilities towards school children.

The holder of the Sailing Master's Certificate will be expected to be able to take charge of a school sailing club, local education authority courses, the organization of regattas and competitions, and of advising head teachers and authorities. The sailing coach will be responsible for the training of sailing masters and instructors, and to the level of ability which should be cogent in directors of authority sailing centres.

The lowest level of certificate, the Dayboat Certificate of the RYA, is planned as a basic introduction to sailing. In spite of its unassuming title many teachers feel that it is still too ambitious a goal for school children. The Scottish School Sailing Association's independence from the NSSA is a political necessity to enable the Scottish Education Department to give financial help to students

109

Figure 15 THE STRUCTURE AND LINES OF
COMMUNICATION FOR THE COACHING SCHEME
FOR SAILING IN BRITAIN

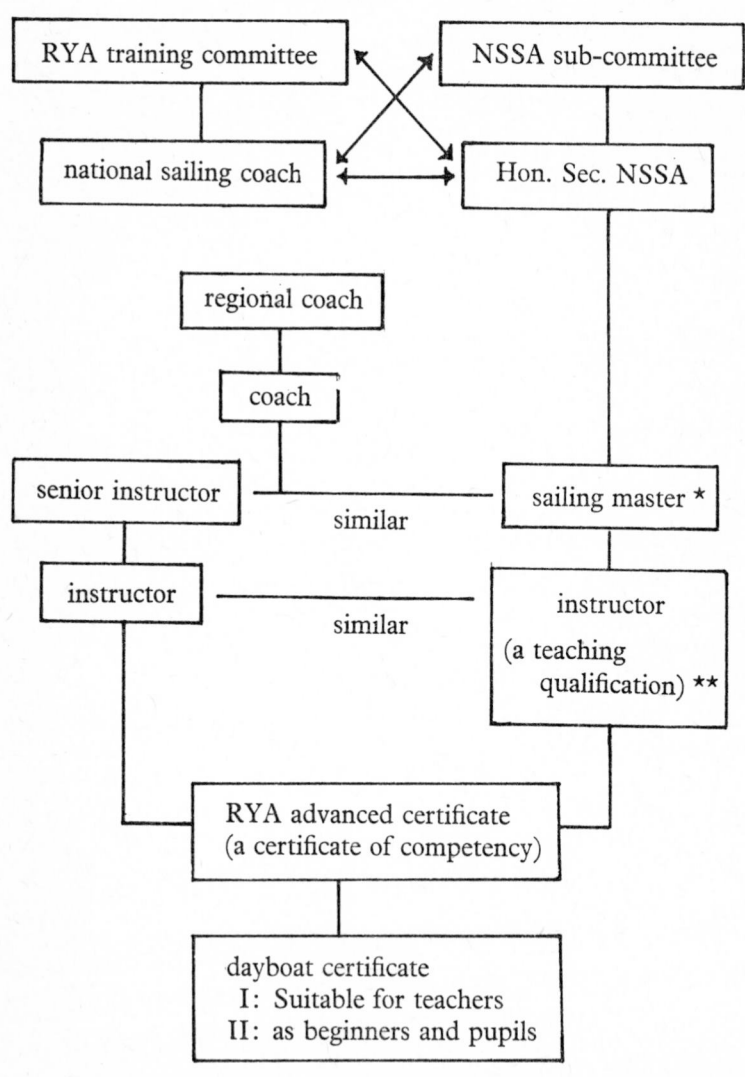

* Formerly the final instructors' certificate (NSSA).
** Formerly the assistant instructors' certificate (NSSA).

on sailing courses in Scotland. The SSSA are concerned about the problems of encouraging absolute beginners, and the Edinburgh section have therefore proposed an even more basic series of proficiency tests as an introduction to the Dayboat Certificate. The three levels proposed are cadet, crew and helm, details of which are included in Appendix H. The risk of accident in inland sailing is not great, and whereas details of fatalities are much documented minor accidents are more difficult to collate.

In summarizing the provision of qualification for outdoor pursuits it is generally true that the most complex schemes of certification are to be seen in those activities with the largest following. The motives for the introduction of certificates serve three principal aims. Firstly, as in the case of the Ski Clubs of Great Britain's Certificates, to afford a status to the holder. Secondly, to provide a means to improved instruction and a more systematic methodology, as in the case of the British Canoe Union. Finally, as in the proposed Caving Instructor's Award and in the Mountain Leadership Certificate, to reduce the inherent hazard in the activities and thus to bring wider acceptance to their educational value.

Since the certificates have been on an *ad hoc* basis, and represent more a response to public demand than a deliberate and centrally directed educational policy, it is not surprising that there is a wide discrepancy between the standards set by governing bodies of the different sports. This tendency is perhaps more noticeable at the lower end of the instructional scale than at the higher end.

It should never be forgotten that although sometimes hazardous the pursuits can be safely instructed by adequately prepared staff. The accident risk can be compared in each of the outdoor pursuits if one assumes that the participants are exposed to risk for similar periods (Fig. 13).

Before considering the role of the teacher in outdoor education and the training for these responsibilities it is relevant to examine the significance which the employers attach to the awards of the governing bodies of sport. Whereas most authorities have for some time insisted on recognized national qualifications for the supervision of swimming there is a certain reluctance to insist on similar qualifications for outdoor education. Considerable misunderstanding has dogged the brief history of such awards, due in part to the confusing nature of their titles. The Mountain Leadership Certificate, for example, is in no way a qualification for the more technical aspects of mountaineering, and indeed is only intended as a minimum acceptable qualification—and even then only under summer conditions. In order to clarify some of these misconceptions it would be useful to indicate those awards which are appropriate for teachers or leaders involved in the normal school programme:

1. Mountain walking (summer). Mountain Leadership Certificate (MLTB + SMLTB).
2. Mountain walking (winter). Winter Mountain Leadership Certificate (SMLTB).
3. Rock climbing. Mountaineering Instructor's Certificate (MLTB + SMLTB).
4. Canoeing. Senior Instructor's Certificate (BCU).
5. Sailing. Instructor's Award (NSSA).
6. Skiing. Ski Party Leader's Certificate (BSIC).
7. Caving. Cave Leader's Certificate (BACI).

There are in addition qualifications available in a wide range of other outdoor pursuits, e.g. orienteering, pony trekking and sub-aqua, and it is likely that a new certificate will emerge for those involved in the leadership of environmental study groups. It is often possible for students in colleges of education to prepare for one of these awards as an integral part of an outdoor education course; and in order to prevent a total fragmentation and unnecessary disparity in these specialized qualifications it is essential that they should continue to be moderated by the national governing bodies of sport. Independent courses at best serve to devalue and debase the existing qualifications, and at worst promote a false security and a positive hazard, and are likely to place both employees in an unenviably invidious position.

The deficiencies of the pre-service training of teachers for outdoor pursuits and outdoor education result largely from a lack of available time within the structured part of a college course. The qualifications of teaching staff, however, play an important part in determining the role of teachers.

At a time when developments in outdoor education are taking place both naturally and by design, serving to simplify understanding of objectives and practices, the role of the instructor and the position of the teacher appear to become more complicated, and for some individuals more uncertain. It is felt that it would be an omission of some magnitude if we did not devote some attention to an appraisal of the present situation which affects those people working in some connection in outdoor education. Also we feel it important to outline what in our opinion are the requirements of a sound specialist instructor.

Why a large number of education authorities considered that an outdoor pursuits or field studies centre operating a hundred miles away would be the most appropriate first step in the growth of interest and expertise in outdoor activity or study in the authorities' schools remains a mystery. However, as has been described earlier, such has been the case, and these centres were staffed by specialists and equipped with specialist equipment and proceeded with their specialist activities. Our concern in this section is solely with the staffing aspect. The Outward Bound Schools, commercially operated centres, trust centres and education centres were, in the main, happy to acquire their staff from amongst the ranks of capable mountaineers, canoeists, skiers, etc., who either had proven experience of instruction or who claimed an interest. Unlike the staff of most field study centres, many of these instructors in outdoor pursuits centres had no appropriate qualifications in either teaching or the activities; the latter were not available.

Of course, some education authorities made it clear that they required, or preferred, a teaching qualification, and often the subject most mentioned, if one was mentioned at all, was physical education. In the absence, still, of any really appropriate teaching qualification for specialists in the field of outdoor education, fashion plays an all too prominent part, and now advertisements for instructors normally call for a qualification in, or knowledge of, environmental studies.

Although many authorities did, and do, not require appointments to be made from amongst qualified teachers, not surprisingly a considerable number of teachers from the widest range of subject

113

disciplines have been attracted to the style of teaching so obvious in outdoor education. It is interesting to find from the statistics produced in the recent survey of Outward Bound schools which are, of course, independent of an education authority or the Department of Education and Science, that of the seventy members of staff of the six schools forty had attended either a college or education or a university.

In order to elaborate even further on the unusual, uncoordinated and perhaps uninformed attitude to the appointment of staff, it is valuable to look at the way authorities pay their instructors. Those authorities which demand a teaching certificate normally pay according to the Burnham scale, but not all do, and the difference in reductions or additions for residential accommodation or duties varies dramatically. Some authorities pay on further education or youth service scales, and others originate their own for specialist instructors regardless of whether they are honours graduates or unqualified in every sense except in experience and enthusiasm. If this latter is the case it is essential to ensure that the scales are both attractive and structured so as to encourage extended service and to offer prospects of promotion.

Most effective centres have, of course, stimulated an awareness of the value of outdoor pursuits and environmental studies in schools, and the hundred-mile geographical gap has been closed noticeably in many instances. The changing emphasis in education has allowed for more recognition to be given to the place of outdoor work in the total education of all children, and it is now apparent that as one of its functions the outdoor centre should be seen as a servicing agency to the requirements of the authority and its schools and not an establishment very much on the sidelines of educational thought and processes.

This different approach brings attendant problems. It is not the intention of this section of the book to foresee the future, or even pronounce on what the authors think should be put into effect; those problems are for later. The present situation is complex enough and needs to be outlined. We have established that the instructors who are in centres or authority based are often teachers whose subject training has only unwittingly fitted them for appointment to a specialist outdoor pursuits centre. Many are not teachers, but their accumulated experience and their instinctive knowledge of the requirements of young people fit them admirably for the role of a specialist instructor. This is, in principle, the present situation, but it would appear that it cannot remain for long.

Many authorities are now embarking upon extended in-service training programmes for teachers, and asking for activity qualifications in order to increase the number of opportunities available to young people to explore and understand the countryside knowledgeably and safely. In many instances teachers are taking over the role of the instructor and there is, logically, a demand for an even greater expertise amongst instructors, a sharpening of centre activity, and an extension in some cases of the requirements made by schools and teachers of both centres and instructors.

There is growing importance attached to the intrinsic value of the activities themselves, an insistence that young people are made aware of the problems which the countryside faces, increased and renewed emphasis upon the personal and social gains from residential and unaccustomed experiences, and a realization that greater benefit will accrue if these processes of education are continuous and progressive, not single, unconnected experiences. The pendulum is beginning to swing and whilst staff at the centres will continue to comment upon, for example, the poor standard of preparation of some of its clientèle, or the disinterest of some teachers or schools, there is evidence that many centres, instructors and activities will be put into question by the increasing number of enthusiastic and experienced teachers. Specialist instructors will have to live up to their specialist role, and the combination of three years' teaching training in outdoor education, and the accumulation of experience, is an inevitable requirement of all specialists, particularly those in the educational field. There is no doubt that there is some disagreement and a great deal of uncertainty surrounding any discussion on the role of an instructor.

Our viewpoint is that although there are differences in technique, varying opportunities and a more flexible environment, the terms 'good teacher' and 'good instructor' are synonymous and from now on the word teacher will be used.

Even though the following exposition of the requirements of a teacher may be thought by some to be theoretical or unreal, it is felt that it is important to produce it in the hope that others will agree with, attain or exceed what we consider to be desirable.

The word 'role' means, in this context, the expected function, performance and behaviour of the individual, and from the

115

diagram it can be seen that the role of a teacher is at least threefold. Every teacher will agree that they have an 'instrumental' function; that is, their responsibility to transmit skills. Many instructors feel that this is what they have been appointed to do, and of course this is the most tangible of the functions to perform and to assess. It is naturally important for teachers to pass on skills, which they must consider themselves fortunate to have had the opportunity to acquire, in an understanding way. Because of the nature of the activities or studies which most instructors are expected to be able to present to their students, and because of the environment and personal involvement in communicating enthusiasm, interest and success (failure is rarely obvious or so damning as it can be in many other academic or practical areas), it is very difficult not to accept the teacher's role to be extended to include an 'expressive' element.

It must be stated at this point that it is very simple to expect a complexity of roles for teachers without regard to certain practical considerations. The most obvious of these are listed in Fig. 16, but probably the most important is the time factor. Outward Bound courses apart, many visits to centres or school camps last at the longest for fourteen days, so it must be borne in mind that the almost peripatetic nature of the teacher's role in this period of time will often only allow for the teacher to go a short way beyond the transmission of skills, and to judge any student on his or her response to the teacher and the activity.

The 'expressive' role does, however, take two forms, the unconscious and the deliberate. Even in the very shortest of times young people will try to emulate their teacher in perhaps dress, mannerism, and even equipment and style. If the activity is presented thoughtfully, then it is unavoidable that through it the recipients will be led to a broadening of experiences which encompasses relationships with others in the group, awareness of future possibilities and probably the beginning of a development of values. If these semi-unconscious factors are present it is as well to remember that the unconcerned teacher will have just as much effect upon the students, but in an unproductive and possible damaging way. If exposure to the activity, to the teacher, to the new environment, is increased then extension of the role can become more deliberate. Parker in *An Approach to Outdoor Activities* says:

'It is far too optimistic to expect great qualities to emerge automatically from participation in outdoor activities. However, there is no questioning the claim that an outlet is provided for the emergence of such features as leadership, courage and friendliness. Possibly by providing youngsters with the opportunity they will be given the chance to display qualities of endurance, self-discipline, determination, humility, self-reliance, unselfishness and loyalty. There may be as many occasions when selfishness and other less socially acceptable traits become apparent.'

A combination of the right activity in the right environment with the right teacher will inevitably produce results well beyond that of an excellence in skills, and a good teacher is well aware of the potential of the situation.

The third role of any teacher can be described as 'organizational', and entails an awareness of the necessity for order, for certain rules and the effects they could have on the reputation of the teacher's establishment. Whilst this is an important function it can be seen that an over-emphasis upon organizational efficiency, whilst conceivably assisting instrumental objectives, is likely to be incompatible with expressive roles because of the necessity amongst the latter for self-expression. The role of a teacher is therefore at least manifold (Fig. 16) and, although dependent upon circumstances, almost always complex. How best can the teacher fulfil all the roles?

It is as well to guard against three well-meaning practices which we often witnessed in outdoor education teaching which hinder educational processes. It is very easy for a teacher to become enthralled by his or her own performance or subject, and to become totally unaware of the standard of requirements of the group, let alone an individual within it. Closely related is the danger of becoming completely committed to beliefs in an activity or study and pouring them upon the heads of those who might not want to know, or who are incapable at that point in time of being equally involved. Thirdly, there is the temptation to submerge the many facets of group activity in a plethora of teachers, often on the grounds of safety. Nothing is more likely to cause greater chaos and, paradoxically, a decrease in value.

The good teacher has been described as a 'facilitator, collaborator and consultant', and therefore should establish an affinity with his group, study and evaluate the individuals in it, assess their

117

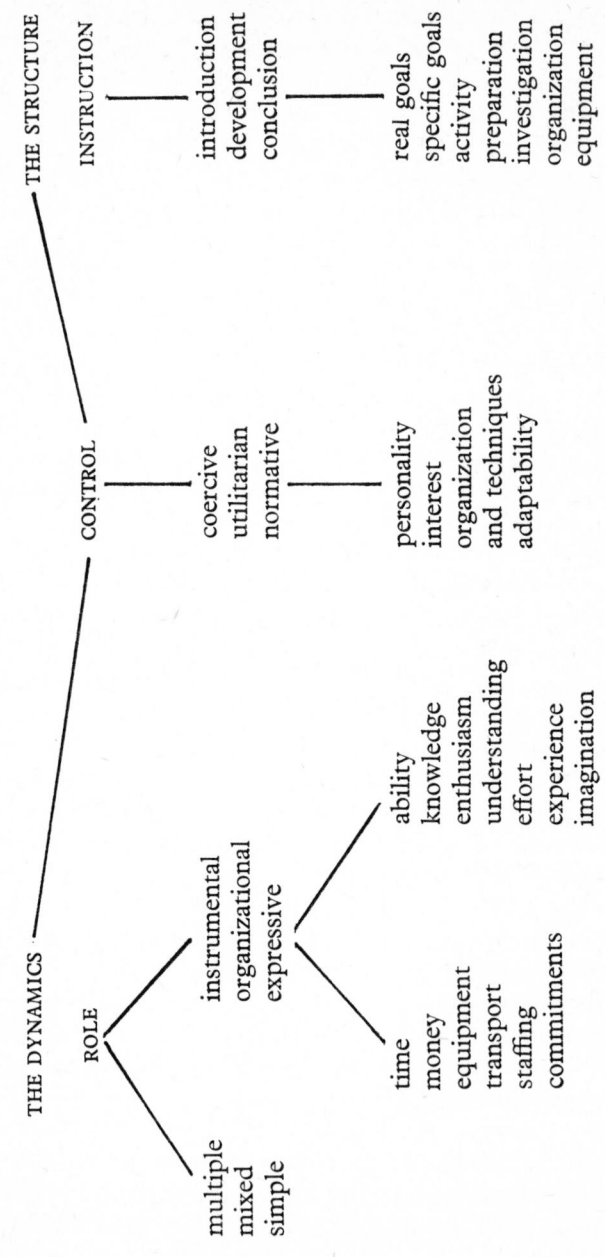

Figure 16 THE ROLE AND REQUIREMENTS OF A TEACHER OR INSTRUCTOR

THE DYNAMICS

ROLE

multiple
mixed
simple

instrumental
organizational
expressive

time
money
equipment
transport
staffing
commitments

ability
knowledge
enthusiasm
understanding
effort
experience
imagination

THE STRUCTURE

CONTROL

coercive
utilitarian
normative

personality
interest
organization
and techniques
adaptability

INSTRUCTION

introduction
development
conclusion

real goals
specific goals
activity
preparation
investigation
organization
equipment

abilities and attitudes, and in an understanding and thoughtful way nurture what he considers commendable. Having begun to build up a mental dossier on the groups the teacher is in a strong position to present his activity in the most appropriate way in terms of learning the skills and of extending each individual whilst providing success, generating enthusiasm, improving confidence and providing scope for imagination, invention, exploration and self-expression within the bounds laid down firmly but with understanding.

Whilst these broad guidelines might be accepted by many teachers, it is impossible to go into a detailed analysis of individual approaches to the task of teaching; it is not so difficult to outline aims, objectives, organization and method of instructional sessions, even though these will differ extensively in detail. As shown in Fig. 16 the mental process behind lessons should encompass the 'real goals' which establish the broad philosophy and purpose behind the work to be embarked upon, and also that the role of the teacher should be instrumental, expressive and organizational.

'Specific goals' can be more clearly defined if only because they can be attempted over a shorter period of time, i.e. one session, and they cover an area to which resources and activity are immediately directed and a result likely to be produced. The activity is chosen to suit the real and specific goals perfectly, but it is obvious on many occasions, especially in the residential centres, that the students must adapt to the activity and the 'goals' are bonuses if everything goes well.

Method and approach are very definitely individual concerns, but an ingredient which is essential and common to all is preparation. Intuition and experience carry the day on a great number of occasions perfectly adequately, but sound preparation of more than just the equipment, transport, etc., is a surer way of producing a balanced teaching activity period. The place of demonstration, questioning, group work, partner activity, individual attention and the all important development of the activity and allocation of time all fit into place, and yet can still be adapted to suit an unforeseen emergent situation.

A conclusion needs to be thought out if the group is to finish on a relevant note, and an evaluation of the success or characteristics of the session is equally important for the teacher in order that he

119

can assess whether the 'specific goals' have been approached, even if not achieved, and that there was some contribution to the 'real goals' at which he was aiming.

Inevitably we have had to sketch over a great deal of the detail which would normally be attributed to the role of the teacher. However, it is hoped that this outline will serve to illustrate the necessity of extensive training and suitable recognition, and the acceptance by instructors of their responsibility and role in the educational field. It is desirable that their formal training is undertaken largely in colleges of education and universities, whose provisions we now examine.

THE TRAINING OF TEACHERS

The divergence in approach to the training and certification of teachers of outdoor pursuits reflects a variety of very different traditions and incentives. In contrast there is a much greater measure of uniformity in the training for environmental subjects. It is not intended that this book should describe in detail the requirements, syllabuses and examination systems which are used in the training of geographers, geologists, botanists, zoologists, meteorologists and climatologists. All of these subjects have great relevance in the field of outdoor education, but taken in isolation they are often too esoteric to be able to make a real contribution to the teaching of outdoor education itself. The essence of outdoor education lies in the integration of these subjects which leads to a full appreciation of the total environment. In this book we are clearly more concerned with the particular environment of the countryside, but it should not be forgotten that to people living in rural communities the problems involved in living in an urban region are as difficult to appreciate as are those of the country for the townsman, and the fact that many more live in towns inevitably means that the problems of the countryside are highlighted by increasing use and in many cases by over-use.

Although most of the British universities offer degree courses in some of the biological or earth sciences there are an increasing number who also offer courses in conservation and related subjects. The Council for Nature listed Aberdeen, the University

College of North Wales, Durham, Edinburgh, East Anglia and University College, London. Of these the new University of East Anglia offers the widest choice of environmental subjects. Although new, the school is popular and takes some hundred undergraduates a year, these being drawn from both arts and science candidates. The first term of the course is essentially a preliminary introduction which not only makes provision for orientating arts students towards the sciences, but also enables students to select their options from some experience of the subjects. Careers in conservation and natural history are limited and the best qualification is a general degree in biological sciences followed by postgraduate work in conservation or biology. East Anglia are at pains, however, to point out that such qualifications cannot replace practical experience which is best gained through the activities of an amateur naturalist society.

The colleges of education in Britain are not only aware of the problems of the environment but are also conscious of the change in emphasis which has occurred in education. Many of the colleges and all of those which have physical education courses offer some training in outdoor pursuits. The extent of this provision varies enormously, but few of them have sufficient time in their normal college programme to do more than introduce students to some of the outdoor pursuits, to make them aware of the dangers involved, to introduce them to organizations which can help in their training and to provide certificates. This continued training is available through a variety of media, but we believe that it is best achieved through LEA in-service training courses, an example of which is provided in Appendix I. Typical of the provision for outdoor education in colleges is the course offered at Bingley College of Education. Three quite distinct courses are offered. The main physical education course in 1968 involved twenty-seven students; twenty-three of these hoped to gain the MLC and seventeen hoped to get a BCU award before leaving college. Without exception they all hoped to establish, and be involved in, outdoor activity groups in their schools. The success of these courses depends to a large measure on the time which can be spared from the more traditional and academic matters of college life. Consequently large parts of the course are undertaken over weekend periods and during vacations. Reference to Fig. 17 shows clearly that some students can find as much as a hundred days a year on which to practise

121

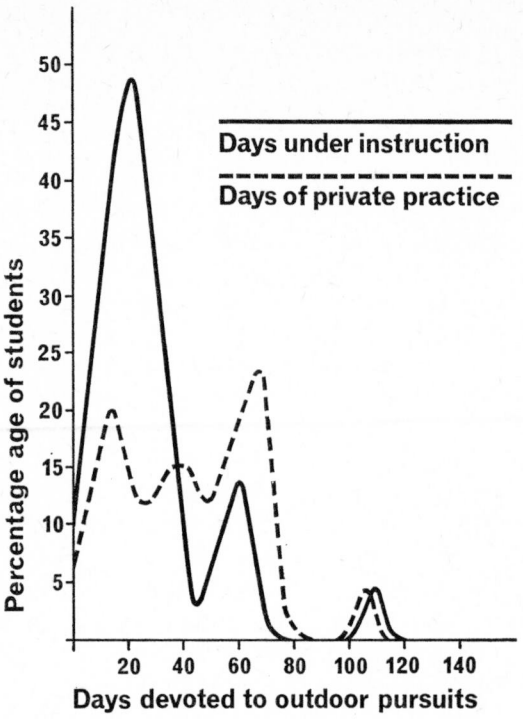

Figure 17   The committed time of students in their final year at Bingley College of Education specializing in outdoor pursuits, 1969.

their skills on their own. Most students receive about thirty days of instruction each year. On examining the popularity of the activities in college courses there is a clear bias towards mountain walking and water sports; the principal reason for this is that these are the most popular activities outside college and they are therefore the activities which are most likely to have appeal in schools. A further point is that both mountain walking and camping, together with canoeing, require neither a great deal of supervision nor a great capital investment. However, one cannot suppress the suspicion that, because these subjects will be examined and assessed, the students devote most time to them. The popularity

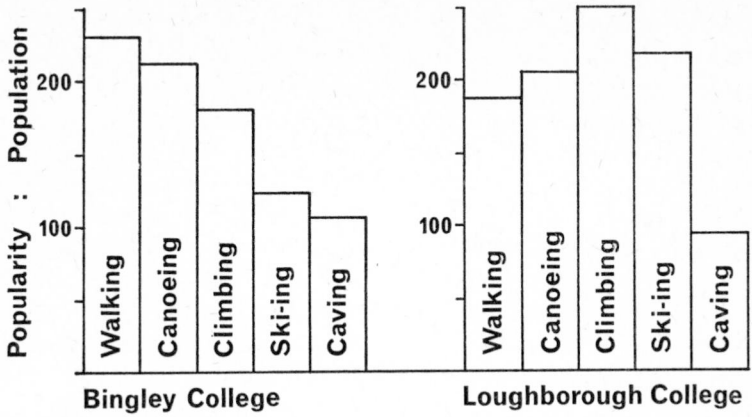

*Figure 18   Popularity of outdoor pursuits at Bingley and Lough-
borough Colleges of Education in 1970—based on scores
of ranked data.*

of the sports as indicated by the Bingley students is shown in Fig.
18 and is in no way atypical of the preference of similar students in
many other colleges. Bingley also includes outdoor pursuits as an
optional subsidiary subject for any student from any department;
a further ninety-four enrolled in this in 1968. Short optional
courses lasting for one term only are also available.

Many of the colleges have their own residential centres, and it
may be worth drawing attention to the organization of the original
residential courses at Loughborough College of Education. Those
lecturers who were responsible for the activities run from Glen
Padarn in Llanberis created a different attitude towards the popularity of activities amongst the students, through their own
enthusiasms and through the situation of the centre. Fig. 18
shows that the specialist skills of canoeing, climbing and skiing
have developed at the expense of mountain walking.

The training of teachers is not the exclusive prerogative of the
colleges of education, and many post-graduates take a one-year
diploma course in a university department of education. As in
the colleges the demands for time for vocational training make it
difficult to offer a complete training in outdoor activities. Of these
university departments Bangor University perhaps comes closest
to approaching their aim of equipping teachers to take a responsible

123

role in outdoor pursuits. This, however, can only be achieved by use of weekends and vacation periods. Part of the student's teaching practice is often undertaken in a residential mountain centre. Typical of the diverse arrangement is the Award Course in Physical Education at Edinburgh University, which also offers a very basic introduction to some outdoor activities. The course is entirely voluntary and covers over two residential courses of one week and two weeks, skiing, mountain walking and a choice from sailing, pony trekking and mountaineering.

The enthusiastic amateur who is catered for by the examinations and tests of the governing bodies of sport is therefore encouraged by most colleges of education and university departments of education to pursue his interests, either with some direction on a purely voluntary basis, or as an integral part of the course.

Outdoor pursuits is not the only subject which is available to the potential teacher of outdoor education. Increasingly colleges of education are offering courses in environmental studies. The subject is obviously too complicated to be dealt with in great depth and the emphasis is placed in quite different directions by different colleges. The courses arranged at I. M. Marsh College of Physical Education in Liverpool have particular relevance to outdoor education because they attempt to bridge the gap between outdoor activities and field studies. A similar integrated course leading to a diploma in outdoor education was started at Moray House College of Education in 1972 (Appendix I). In the former, the course lasts for three years and includes the educational content of a normal teachers' training course. In the latter, the course is available only to those who already hold a teaching or other similar qualification. The success of these courses will depend to a large measure on the support which is given to this type of integrated curriculum in schools.

Just as in the case of outdoor pursuits it is possible to gain the same technical qualifications by either attending a college of education or submitting to assessment as an individual so it is possible to gain experience in the more academic field studies. Regular courses are run by the Field Studies Council at their residential centres such as Malham Tarn and Flatford Mill. The Royal Society for the Protection of Birds has recently embarked on a policy of establishing nature centres where instruction can be given to teachers and adult members of the RSPB.

The increasing demands for recreation in the countryside are for the physical activities, for nature study, scientific work or merely for the satisfaction of the tourist; all are imposing demands which even now need to be controlled. It was with these problems in mind that during the 1960s a number of courses were introduced for management studies with a particular emphasis on recreational aspects.

At present there is one diploma course run by the London Polytechnic and degree courses run by Loughborough and Leeds. The diploma course, of one year, covers in the first part economics, decision making and information technology, sociology and the management of leisure, the management of human behaviour, and the design and operation of recreational centres. The details of the full syllabus are given in Appendix I. The courses at Leeds and Loughborough are very similar to the Diploma of Management Studies and also last for one year, but result in the degree of MSc. At the moment there is no corresponding course for recreational management in Scotland, although the Scottish Education Depart - ment have laid the guide-lines for DMS courses which are flexible, forward looking and realistic—based on co-operation between industry, colleges and students in the important expanding field of management education and training. The plans are sufficiently adaptable to allow for a DMS in recreation.

In summarizing the training facilities for teachers of outdoor education it is clear that in the sphere of outdoor pursuits the technical qualifications are adequately directed by the governing bodies of sport. Those establishments of education who are involved in this work make full use of the existing facilities. It is quite possible for an enthusiastic student to gain awards in all of the outdoor pursuits outside the normal full-time course, whether he is in a college of education or a university, but where training arrangements are made the task is clearly easier. Increasing numbers of colleges recognize a value in outdoor education and have made it possible for students to gain some introduction to the interests of their choice.

Although an interest in outdoor education has been generated it is of particular interest to examine how such an interest could be fostered under the new proposals for the training of teachers recommended in the James Report. In an attempt to overcome the diversity of the teaching profession the report advocated a four-year training period for all teachers. The present fragmentation of study courses means that 'theoretical study is often undertaken at the expense of practical preparation for first teaching assignments'. In order to achieve the adequate preparation it is proposed that there should be three cycles.

The first cycle would be primarily concerned with personal higher education which may be either a university or polytechnic degree course, possibly containing an element of educational study for students who are already vocationally motivated towards the teaching profession. Acceptable higher education would also be provided through the new two-year Diploma of Higher Education (Dip HE). The diploma, like the degree course, may contain an educational bias. One-third of the time would be devoted to general studies, the remaining two-thirds would be divided between two elected main subjects. The Dip HE would not be exclusively a teacher's qualification but would provide the necessary higher educational background for entry to a wide variety of professions, or give entry to a university degree course. Within this first cycle it is clear that the opportunities exist, particularly in the context of the general course, to promote an awareness of the environment through a general course in countryside appreciation. Such a course would not only provide an insight into the problems of conservation and countryside recreation, but could also open many unknown avenues which could be further explored at degree level. There are also opportunities to involve students in a more specialized knowledge of the environment through main course subjects. If the colleges of education do become the principal agency for the Dip HE the opportunities for the advancement of outdoor education will be immense.

The second cycle for teacher training is split into two years; the first of these is concerned with professional training within a college of education or university department of education and the second year is spent as a licensed teacher working in a school. The licensed teacher's programme would be condensed and there would be continuation courses run in the training establishment for discussion, seminars and the supervision of project work. After satisfactory completion of the teaching year the licensed teacher becomes a recognized teacher and is awarded the degree of BA (Educ.). The B.Ed would become a further degree following an in-service training period. The M.Ed would be retained as a research degree in education. The year spent in college during the second cycle could include a main subject in outdoor education, and licensed teachers specializing in this field might expect to spend some of their time teaching in either residential centres, or with schools where there was an existing interest in outdoor education.

The third cycle provides an increased opportunity for in-service training and might eventually provide the means for releasing registered teachers for one full term for every five years of service completed. The intention is to give teachers an opportunity to remain informed of changes in educational practice and thought, and at the same time to allow them to widen their teaching experience and interests. Within this third cycle there would be many opportunities to run specialized certificate or diploma courses, and with the increase in concern expressed by education authorities it seems inevitable that outdoor education courses will provide the right opportunities for teachers to gain the skills, knowledge and philosophy which will enable them to make a valuable contribution.

The administrative structure of the colleges and the granting of the new degrees would become the ultimate responsibility of a new organization, the National Council for Teacher Education and Training (NCTET), which in turn would be regionalized through the Regional Councils for Colleges and Departments of Education (RCCDE). The RCCDEs would be based on the new regional areas and would provide a closer link between all centres of higher education within each region; in particular they would co-ordinate the provision for teacher training, and by interpretation of the requirements of the NCTET would assess the numbers who could continue to the second cycle of teacher training.

The demand for teachers is now almost satisfied, and even the additional staff required in the school to cope with the increase of the school leaving age and the implementation of the third cycle of the James Report will mean that the resources of the colleges of education may be under-used. The introduction of the Dip HE would make appropriate use of the recent expansion of the colleges and would allow for further expansion. Such a situation could result in educational innovations which may be easier to implement in a period of expansion than in one of stagnation or contraction.

Training teachers in outdoor education has until recently been too often regarded as an elective course and the time available for instruction has been severely limited by lack of programmed time. Much of the work has of necessity been undertaken at weekends and during vacations. In order to provide the opportunities that this branch of education merits it is essential that outdoor education should be regarded as a main subject in the college curriculum. Opportunities for qualified teachers to further their interest in outdoor education are best served by comprehensive one-year courses leading to an acceptable national diploma, such as that offered by Moray House. The resources of the national outdoor pursuits centres do not equip them to undertake this task satisfactorily, although they have a significant contribution to make within the courses offered by the colleges. One term in-service courses such as those offered recently by Plas-y-Brenin and Dunfermline College, although making a significant contribution, should not be regarded as isolated experiences but should be structured into a broader concept of training.

The examples cited throughout this section illustrate the extensive interest shown in outdoor education, but at the same time underline the need for a greater degree of cohesive centralized development.

CURRICULUM AND EXAMINATION DEVELOPMENTS

The previous section has shown how training in a wide variety of colleges and universities, and over an equally wide range of subject matter, has attempted to aid teachers capable of taking part in interdisciplinary and related studies programmes. The need for this approach has been recognized for many years, but it is only since the adoption of comprehensive education on a wide scale, and the breaking down of some of the traditional academic barriers, that it has been possible to implement the concept of related studies programmes through team teaching. With the introduction of the Certificate of Secondary Education (CSE) and the SCE in Scotland it has been possible to provide an element of academic responsibility to subjects which previously would not have been recognized. The CSE examinations still represent a lower grade of qualification than the General Certificate of

Education at the 'O' level, as is shown by the fact that only top grades in the CSE examinations are recognized as equivalent to 'O' levels. In many respects the syllabus for CSE as it affects outdoor education is more satisfactory; much of the programme is devoted to project work which provides, even at a very introductory level, opportunities for elementary research and demonstrates the relationship between cause and effect. Inevitably the higher ranking GCE examinations attract the more academic students whereas the CSE, if not exactly a sop to the less intellectually gifted, is nevertheless better suited to their requirements. The development of the Mode III section of the CSE in which a syllabus can be formulated by a school and approved by one of the examining boards has great benefits. The syllabus can be tailored to match the enthusiasm of the teachers and to fit both the interests of the students and the facilities of the environment.

Not all of the outdoor education offered in schools is orientated to the passing of examinations, indeed this at the moment is the exception. More generally it is regarded as a legitimate alternative to the traditional aspects of education.

The public schools, where students' time can more easily be directed, were among the first to make use of outdoor pursuits. In many cases this manifested itself in a shift away from the paramilitary training offered through the Combined Cadet Force. During the 1950s the demands imposed by conscription were met through the auspices of the CCF, but with the cessation of conscription this concept was largely invalidated with a consequent shift in emphasis from pre-military training towards ideals of character building through arduous training. The popularity of this work is illustrated by the case of Marlborough College, where arduous training became so divorced from pre-military training that an expeditions master was appointed with responsibility for arranging courses of outdoor activities not only during the term but also during the vacations. This had already happened at Gordonstoun, but it indicates the shift in emphasis which can be brought about by changes in political circumstances and through minor adjustments in the attitude of society.

In the previous chapter (also appendices) some details of school outdoor education programmes are described, but it is now relevant to look at one in particular, that of Abbotsholme School. The traditions of Abbotsholme have always been towards a liberal education and certainly in the field of outdoor education they remain as progressive as they were at the turn of the century. The syllabus for each of the four years of secondary education at Abbotsholme is included in Appendix J. The course for boys and girls is a compulsory aspect of school work, but it is not assessed directly for external examinations. In the public sector of education it often proves difficult to offer a course in outdoor education running right through the secondary school career and more often it is restricted to specific years. In the case of the GCE syllabuses pressures of academic work leave little time for non-examination subjects; consequently any introduction to outdoor pursuits is offered either at the age of fourteen or during the first term in the lower sixth form. Both of these are terms when the pressure of academic work is least acute. In the case of the less gifted students the final year at school is often taken as the period for an introduction to outdoor pursuits, not because academic pressures are less but more because there is the perennial problem of occupying the time of reluctant school attenders and every attempt is made to whet their rather jaded appetite for traditional school subjects.

Experiments have been made in running CSE Mode III examinations for a wide variety of subjects, which by definition fall within the sphere of outdoor education. A CSE course in outdoor pursuits provides an introduction to the physical aspects of a variety of outdoor activities, but through a study of expedition accounts and biographies provides an understanding of the problems, purposes and philosophies of expeditions and the personalities involved. The field is narrow and it is likely that some of the Mode III programmes which have been used in Northumberland will become widely adopted. The authority was among the first to appoint an organizer of outdoor education and a number of old rural schools have been converted for use as field study centres. Typical of this is the Howtel Centre which was adapted from a former primary school. The approach to the environment and the consequent content of CSE Mode III curricula are determined largely by the situation of the school. Whatever the approach, outdoor pursuits as such are never examined in isolation but only in so far as they contribute to a full understanding of the environment and the ability to live in remote areas. It is the fruits of exploration that are considered examinable. The related studies programme uses the natural environment to provide a thread of continuity for a wide range of subjects. It includes geography, biology, English, history, art and folklore, and in each case the students are involved in co-operative projects. A syllabus typical of related studies is that of Gosforth East County Secondary School.

More academic courses are run in the selective schools and it is interesting to note that the CSE Mode III examination in environmental studies is found to allow a more imaginative approach than the definitive syllabus of the 'O' levels. A typical two-year syllabus for CSE Mode III in environmental studies is that of Longbenton High School in Northumberland.

Preparation for more specialized work in outdoor education is covered by work programmes on social studies covering the middle school years from nine to thirteen. Although not an examination subject *per se*, such a course attempts to bring about a systematic extension of the child's knowledge of the environment, which in turn brings about an awareness of the consequences of change. Through an essentially practical approach the course maintains a continuity of enlightenment throughout middle school life. As a result of ranging widely over a variety of related subjects children can arrive at an open-ended situation where at thirteen they are capable of probing some of these fields in greater depth.

The divergence in interpretation of the environment and the significant variations in the environment itself inevitably means that courses will be very different. With few exceptions there is an attempt to familiarize students with the problems of pollution and conservation, and to awaken in them a total awareness of the manifestly different aspects of the environment. The popularity of these types of courses, not only with the teachers involved but also with the pupils, suggests that the increasing number of courses run by colleges of education and university education departments are serving not only an existing need, but one which is likely to become even more pressing.

Chapter Four

BIBLIOGRAPHY

BEAZELEY E. *The Countryside on View*. Constable, 1972.

CARPENTER P. *The Outward Bound Schools; a means of assessment of character*. Ph.D. Oxford University, 1961.

FLETCHER B. *Report on the Outward Bound Schools*. Bristol University, 1970.

MELDRUM K. I. *Mountain Activity Instructors' Certification*. M.Phil. Thesis. Nottingham University, 1970.

PARKER T. *An Approach to Outdoor Activities*. Pelham, 1970.

PATMORE J. A. *Land and Leisure*. David & Charles, 1970.

SILLITOE K. K. *Planning for Leisure*. HMSO, 1971.

Wolfenden Report. CCPR, 1960.

LORD JAMES. *Report on Teacher Training*. HMSO, 1971.

British Mountaineering Council Committee Minutes.

Mountain Leadership Training Board's. Records 1964–1972.

Mountain Rescue Committee. Accident statistics.

Pilot National Recreation Survey. Keele University and British Travel Association, 1969.

A comparative study of outdoor education

Although it would be possible to predict likely future trends in the development of outdoor education based on the impetus which the movement has already generated in Britain, it is relevant to examine the provisions in other countries, particularly the United States and selected countries in Europe. By means of comparative studies it is possible to show that progress in Britain is in some ways unique, but that many of the trends are seen as clearly in other countries. It is certainly true that different educational policies, distinct environments and national traits colour the emphasis which is placed on the various component elements that make up the broad field of outdoor education. Whereas provisions existing in one country may adequately fulfil the needs of that society, it is unrealistic to consider adopting any modifications without a detailed knowledge of the aims and aspirations which society expects from outdoor education. For example, the fact that most Austrian school children have opportunities to ski should not be used in an argument that the same situation should necessarily be encouraged in Britain. Nor could Icelandic or Swedish charac-teristics be expected to occur say in America. The long dark nights in Iceland make it very difficult to develop outdoor education despite the unique environment, outstanding features and the desire of educationalists to do so. In the summer the pony is used for trekking, but mainly as a means of transport, and should the harvest, the shearing and the fish shoals require attention then school children contribute to the work force.

Scandinavia's family approach to skiing and orienteering is, of course, a significant feature in their approach to outdoor education. It is in Sweden and Norway that this very effective way of introducing young people to a love of the countryside and catering for their continued interest through the family is best exemplified. For the sake of consistency the role of environmental studies and outdoor pursuits will be considered separately before reviewing the attitudes and trends in outdoor education.

Considering the environmental approach first it should be stressed that there is nothing new in the concept of using the environment as a teaching medium. Long ago Decroly advocated environmental studies as a means of inducing children to 'observe, associate and express'. The place which is assigned to the study of the environment varies, but in a UNESCO report of 1968 it was found that the majority of countries not only in Europe, but throughout the world, did not generally regard it as a valid subject in its own right. Of those countries which did make provision in their schools for environmental studies the analysis of the subjects included under this heading gave the following rank order of subjects:

1. Geography.
2. Nature study.
3. History.
4. Civics (social and ethical education).
5. Health education.
6. Mother tongue and literature.
7. Social studies (geography, civics and sociology).
8. Arts (folklore, music, etc.).
9. Biology (especially ecology).
10. Agriculture (and rural science).
11. Languages.
12. Arithmetic and mathematics.
13. Physical education.
14. Religion.
15. Training for safety.

It is hardly surprising that the three at the top of the list embrace most of the subjects which in Britain are generally regarded as field studies, and which between them cover most of the material aspects of the environment. Because of their precise nature they lend themselves as subjects more readily to a clear-cut understanding, and through their necessary interdependence offer a convenient means of relating subjects. The human study of the environment is equally obviously not such a precise science, and requires a more sophisticated approach to appreciate the significance of the relationships between people and the environment. The encyclopedic range of subjects reflects the needs of particular societies. In the less technologically advanced countries it will be readily appreciated how the environmental emphasis comes to be placed on agriculture. In the case of countries whose folk culture is in danger of submergence there is concern for the maintenance of folklore, traditional music and art. Just as environmental studies, as a subject, is not mentioned in the list, neither is outdoor pursuits. The low ranking of physical education, perhaps the subject most expected to be linked, gives some indication of the measure of importance likely to emerge from an examination of outdoor pursuits in the educational context.

The two most important factors in the promotion of environmental studies are the type and availability of the environment and the educational philosophy which promotes the importance of the subject, together with the educational administration which implements it. By selecting countries in Europe whose natural environment is very different and whose educational administration is either centralized or decentralized, it is possible to provide a useful framework for comparison. The countries selected are Belgium, France, Switzerland and Britain. Both France and Belgium have a strongly centralized educational system and yet have quite different mountain environments. Britain and Switzerland are, in contrast, decentralized but again their environment is very different. The United States cannot so readily be compared because of its difference in size and the range of its environment, but because so many of the aspects of recreational sociology which have developed there have appeared subsequently in Europe, it is important to examine their provision as well as the European countries before considering the future of outdoor education in Britain.

ENVIRONMENTAL STUDIES

At one extreme is the attitude in Belgium which accepts the role of environmental studies only in so far as it serves to stimulate an interest in other more traditional school subjects. There is no question of studying the environment for its own sake. The related studies approach to the environment is felt to be more appropriate at the primary level of education. The training of teachers reflects these attitudes and it is only in the final year's training of geography teachers that an introduction to the teaching of field studies is offered. Students training to teach science and geography in lower secondary schools devote five days each year to study tours.

It is surprising that the attitudes in France should be so different when in so many respects the Belgian educational patterns and traditions are based on those of France. Although environmental studies find no place in the baccalauréat examination, and indeed experiments to introduce an environmental content during the year preceding the examination in some progressive and experimental lycées have met with disapproval, there is nevertheless a strong emphasis on this approach during the période d'orientation. As early as 1945 the word 'environment' occurs in official syllabuses, and one of the ministry circulars of 1964 stresses that pupils must be brought into contact with problems in their area and shown how the physical, social, financial and psychological factors in most of these problems are interrelated. The circular goes on to point out that 'this will enlarge their general education and teach them to observe, analyse and criticize, allow them to sympathize and give them an appreciation of humanity and of human fellowship.' In spite of the importance which is attached to environmental education during the transition period, much of the more advanced work is undertaken in the form of supplementary activities run through school co-operatives or social educational schools clubs. The general exception to this rule are the outdoor sessions of the classes de neige and the more recent classes de plein air where, apart from the outdoor pursuits which are inspired by the terrain, the formal teaching which forms an integral part of the classes is directed towards an appreciation of the new environment.

Switzerland takes the opposite extreme to the view in Belgium. With the strong educational tradition based on the teaching of Pestalozzi, Rousseau and Father Girard, it is not surprising that emphasis should be placed on the value of the holistic environmental approach.

In the primary schools of Valais, and this is no exception to the attitude in other cantons, the aim is 'to educate the children, and this can best be done by steeping all instruction in the life around them and by a study of the environment'. The dominating nature of the Swiss mountain environment and its concomitant factors of isolation have resulted in a greater awareness of the importance of nature. This attitude is perhaps more clearly seen in the field of outdoor pursuits than in environmental education, where no special provisions are made simply because the teaching is seen in the context of Rousseau's naturism. The general attitude in the secondary schools places increasing emphasis on the formal scientific interpretation of environmental studies. Co-operation between the youth organizations and the schools is often lacking in spite of the fact that there are complementary features in their work and objectives. Although this situation pertains generally in Europe, elsewhere there is a more marked degree of integration. The American schools, for example, actively encourage their students to join youth groups, and in Bulgaria almost every school is sponsored by a firm or factory, and groups of the Dimitrov Union of Communist Youth arrange courses for pupils ranging from production to artistic evenings and courses on folklore and the environment.

In the United States of America there is an unambiguous emphasis placed on environmental conservation within the provision for outdoor education. It is difficult to compare the practices within a country ranging over such vast areas and whose environment ranges from tropical forests to Arctic mountains. The problem is further aggravated by the decentralization of the educational provision throughout the individual states. Since the Second World War there has been increasing concern over the preservation of the environment, but even since the foundation of the world's first national park at Yellowstone in 1876, there has been a concern for the preservation of wilderness regions. The National Parks Service of the Department of the Interior is the agency through which the many national parks are administered. The principal concern within the parks is the preservation of resource integrity and severe constraints are imposed not only on the total number of visitors but also on the diversity of their activities. Recreation within the parks is regarded as something of a necessary evil. In spite of this, the national parks make provision through the Concessions Policy Act of 1965 for the establishment of well-organized recreational facilities. Concessions are granted to approved

137

agencies for the promotion of specialist recreational activities. These concessions may be granted to those agencies offering the highest tender for the rights but the service is not obliged to accept the highest offer. Concessionaires are expected to provide their own buildings to approved standards; such a capital investment makes it difficult to replace the concessionaires and the service's new policy is to provide the amenities themselves and to lease these to approved agents. These agencies are clearly commercially orientated, but although instruction, equipment, kit hire and guided expeditions are profit motivated, they are none the less well organized. Individuals taking part in specialized activities outside the control of the agencies are required to report to the park ranger's office and obtain a special use permit. The money available for the administration of national parks may be reallocated as a result of recent boundary discussions in such a way that regions are determined by demographic rather than geographic criteria. The resulting redistribution of finance, if implemented, would be likely to restrict the funds available for park administration.

The National Parks Service is concerned with its responsibility for the promotion of environmental appreciation, particularly since the remoteness of many of the national parks for many people makes visits at least irregular, if they can be afforded at all. A scheme to involve young people in their local environment has recently been introduced. Whereas the national parks are more concerned with environmental preservation and regard recreation as something of a fringe benefit, the areas designated as national recreation areas place the emphasis on the recreational amenities, and promote these with a regard to conservation where this is compatible. Ski lifts and competition skiing, for example, are not permitted in a national park but would be actively promoted in a recreation area. In order to satisfy recreational demands, most of the designated areas are sited within easy reach of relatively large populations. Within the Department of Agriculture, the Forestry Service is conscious of its responsibilities for providing access and recreation. Although the service does not directly provide any amenities like the Parks Service, they can grant concessions for trail riding, canoeing, car parking and accommodation within the areas they manage.

All the provisions for recreation are provided as a result of exhaustive research into demand and potential demand and with due regard to the cost benefit analyses of the exercise. Such a rigorous treatment often means that facilities are provided from the top, unlike Britain where provisions are more normally made as a direct response to clearly defined and strongly expressed aspirations from the potential users themselves.

Although there is a widely expressed concern for environmental preservation, many other opportunities to introduce young people to the countryside are lost. University courses for practising teachers are emerging largely, one suspects, because of the concern for conservation, population and pollution prevalent in America rather than an awareness of the total educational value of outdoor education. The summer camp schools taking young people from the age of five upwards for a period of two months would provide an unrivalled opportunity to promote all aspects of outdoor education. That they fail to achieve this in many aspects is due to their being commercially orientated. Many parents regard the summer camp as a heaven-sent opportunity to pack off the children for the summer, leaving them free to take a holiday alone. In order to justify the camps on educational grounds, aspects of social activity are emphasized. That many children return regularly, and themselves become camp councillors, indicates that in spite of the underlying philosophies involved, camp schools are nevertheless an enjoyable experience.

The Outward Bound schools which only run during the summer months are, like the summer camps, planned to give students an opportunity to relate socially. Although undeniably arduous, not all the schools stress the importance of community service, nor do they provide the opportunities to develop specialist skills as in the European Outward Bound schools.

The popularity of apparently hazardous outdoor pursuits is not so great as in the other countries examined. Whereas participation in both sailing and skiing is increasing enormously, there is not a comparably high interest shown in mountaineering, caving and canoeing. It is tempting to suggest that the psychological needs which these hazardous pursuits satisfy in the European context are met in America by more material status symbols. Although it is difficult to generalize, the wide diversity of provisions springs from a lack of overall co-ordination and a failure to appreciate the educational potential of outdoor education.

In each of the countries so briefly mentioned the aims and definitions of environmental studies reflect sociological, political and educational aspirations. The full range of aims is given by UNESCO as:

1. Ensuring pupils' active participation in teaching by observation and experience.
2. Basing teaching on concrete ideas.
3. Providing a better introduction to certain subjects.
4. Development of appreciation and respect of nature.
5. Facilitating children's adjustment to other surroundings.
6. Providing a link between home and school backgrounds.
7. Helping to improve living conditions, housing, hygiene, nutrition.
8. Encouraging collective work and forming an introduction to social education.
9. An introduction to the phenomena of contemporary society and economic life.
10. An aid to school guidance.
11. Fostering international understanding.

The most common objectives listed are to provide a form of coherent education as a whole which attempts to bridge the widening gaps between schools and everyday life by fostering a sense of social and civic responsibility on a regional, national and international basis. In view of the remarkable degree of international accord which environmental education elicits, it is perhaps surprising to find that the principal stumbling-blocks to its wider application are the fundamental lack of appropriate general textbooks and the failure to train specialist teachers. The solution to the problem of providing environmental teachers is normally found by offering an introduction to the subject in teachers' training colleges and by offering subsequent in-service courses served by educational information and equipment centres.

OUTDOOR PURSUITS

Although there is a measure of agreement in the basic principles of environmental education, there is a less well-formulated policy towards the value of outdoor pursuits. Just as in the case of environmental education, the emphasis which is placed on outdoor recreation in general, and specific activities in particular, is a function of educational, social and political motives and the availability of environments. By examining and interpreting the various attitudes to outdoor pursuits it is possible to define both common and divergent trends. The main philosophies of outdoor pursuits can be seen within those countries whose attitudes towards environmental education have already been examined. The principal aims can be summarized as follows:

1. Development of leadership.
2. Development of desirable personality traits,
   e.g.: (a) initiative, (b) resourcefulness, (c) independence, (d) co-operation, (e) self-realization, (f) perseverance, (g) self-sacrifice.
3. The provision of lasting leisure time recreation.
4. The increases in fitness and health.
5. An introduction to wilderness environments.
6. An opportunity to equip young people with the skills to participate in field work in remote tracts.
7. Training for military service.

The most significant factors in the popularity of any outdoor pursuit are the availability of facilities and the measure of encouragement and support. Selected outdoor pursuits in Belgium, France, Switzerland and Britain serve to illustrate the main trends.

Although the total number of participants in each sport can provide a valuable indication of popularity (Fig. 19), only an examination of popularity trends can provide the information which illustrates the effects of educational policies (Fig. 20). Without exception skiing is the most popular of the mountain activities, and it is important to notice that the popularity is a direct function of distance from the available ski resorts. Two factors are involved here: on the one hand is the additional expense involved in reaching distant facilities and on the other is the self-generating enthusiasm which is developed by proximity to appropriate amenities. Partly because of the tradition of skiing, which had its origin in the leisured middle classes at the turn of last century, and partly because of the expense of skiing, not only in terms of equipment but also in terms of travelling costs and uphill transport, the sport, until the 1960s, remained, if not quite the exclusive preserve of the middle class, then very nearly so. These traditions have been irretrievably broken by the promotional success of commercial ski tour operators, and by the

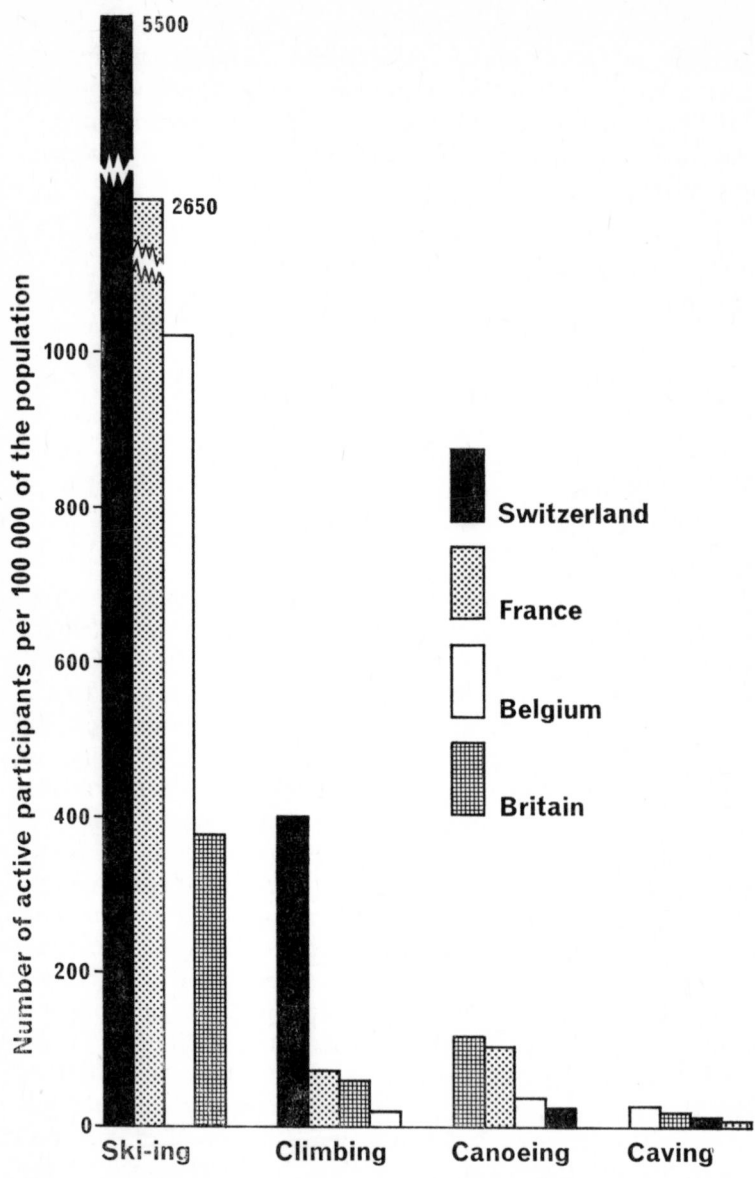

Figure 19   Comparative popularity of selected outdoor activities in some west European countries in 1968.

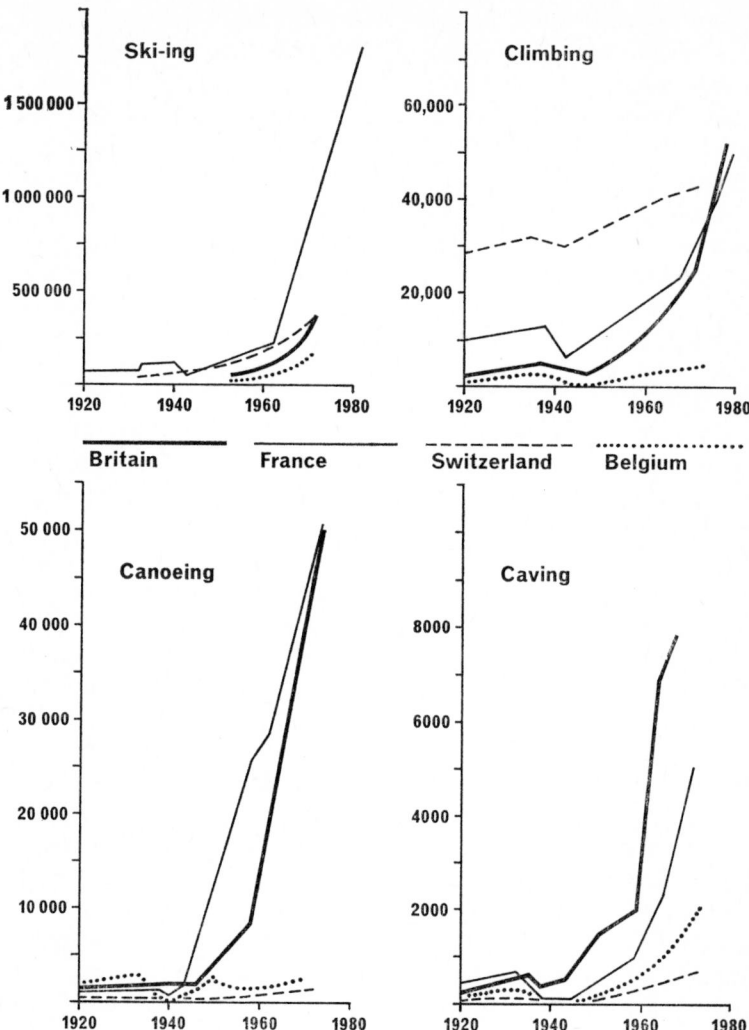

Figure 20 The comparative development of outdoor pursuits in selected European countries.

encouragement which has been afforded in most European countries in the state schools, both at the primary and secondary levels of education.

In France certification for skiing is centralized through the Ministry of Sport. The Ministry is responsible for running a number of regional ski centres under the auspices of the Union des Centres des Activités de Plein Air (UCPA). Considerable encouragement to primary school children is offered by the classes de neige where a whole class, together with the class teacher, visits a ski resort for several weeks. Mornings are devoted to a modified teaching programme which takes advantage of the new environment, while each afternoon is devoted to skiing; no normal schooling is lost. A limited number of places at the UCPA centres are available to young industrial workers who express an interest in the sport and whose quality of work justifies such financial aid. Because of the large and growing number of foreign ski tourists the element of professionalism amongst ski instructors is more firmly legislated for than in other countries. Such legislation is made relatively simple through the means of a National Ski Federation and a centralized sports administration. Through these same agencies a full range of integrated ski teaching certificates is available covering the fields of personal proficiency and both amateur and professional teaching qualifications. The upward surge of interest during the 1960s suggests skiing will be a more popular sport than in other European countries.

Belgium follows very much the pattern of France. The Central Administration of Physical Education and Sport has a range of proficiency and instructing certificates comparable to those of France, with the exception of the professional grades where the demand for ski teachers is limited. The popularity of the sport continues to grow, partly through the introduction of classes de neige and partly through the development of Belgian ski resorts in the Ardennes and the continued promotion of foreign resorts by the ski tour operators.

In Switzerland the situation is rather different, and the very proximity of the ski facilities means that less encouragement is required to inspire school children to take to the snows. During the winter season when other forms of physical education are restricted by the climate to sports hall activities there is every incentive for young people to take part in winter sports.

In general the popularity of mountaineering follows the pattern which might have been predicted, bearing in mind the availability of suitable climbing grounds. Belgium, with resources limited to a few limestone cliffs in the Ardennes, has correspondingly few climbers. At the other extreme Switzerland has a proportionately higher number of climbers. Between these extremes lie Britain and France; in both cases there has been a remarkably similar growth in the sport since the 1950s. In France some encouragement is offered to students to attend holiday courses for mountaineering run by the UCPA, but there is little provision made for climbing as a curricular school activity. The other significant difference lies in the field of certification and training of instructors and guides.

As in the case of skiing the certificates are backed up by law, and no unqualified mountaineer may instruct professionally. The profession of guiding, although viable, is limited, and many guides work as ski instructors in the winter and seek regular employment in the UCPA centres. Both the professional and amateur guides are all trained at the École National de Ski et d'Alpinisme at Chamonix. The greatest opportunities for outdoor education in France are provided by the colonies des vacances which each year involve about a million young people. Leaders are trained through the Centre d'Entraînement aux Méthodes d'Éducation Active (CEMEA). Such leaders who have also gained qualifications in skiing and climbing can be apprenticed to the centres of the Union des Centres de Plein Air (UCPA), where their further educational and professional training is provided. The colonies des vacances, unlike the American summer camps, are not profit motivated, but the wide age range catered for makes it difficult to provide much more than a subsidized holiday in an agreeable environment and, at the same time, afford an experience in supervised leadership for some of the older students. In spite of the relative lack of encouragement which is offered for climbing in France, the growth in popularity is comparable to that in Britain where considerably greater encouragement is offered. We are therefore slightly suspicious of the exaggerated claims for the promotion of the pursuit as a lasting interest which is claimed by some British educationalists. It seems that throughout western Europe there is an inexorable trend towards this type of activity, which owes as much to changing social conditions as to other more direct promotional media.

In Switzerland the majority of mountaineering instruction, particularly at the junior level, is arranged by the junior section of the Swiss Alpine Club (CAS). Each year the various regional sections of the club can receive a training grant from the central committee. The dangers of introducing novices to the mountains are fully appreciated by Swiss teachers who, because of problems of insurance, would never take out students from their schools; the only exception to this rule is in the case of teachers who are also qualified mountain guides. Apart from the courses of the CAS, some mountaineering has been included as an optional aspect of the work of the Éducation Physique de Gymnastique et Sports which is a form of pre-military training. The most recent move has been to demilitarize the EPGS courses and to make them available to girls. Conscription for residents in the remote mountains frequently includes an introduction to alpine warfare, which in turn provides an introduction to mountaineering. It is agreed by most Swiss educationalists that mountaineering should be a recreation which is freely available to all, but that participation should be entirely voluntary. The Swiss have too great a regard for the unpredictability and danger of mountains to coerce reluctant débutantes to take part in pursuits which involve significantly greater objective dangers than the mountains of Britain.

The scheme of mountain certification in Belgium seems to be over-elaborate considering the number of climbers, but their unique contribution lies in the field of personal proficiency assessment. Young mountaineers can attend courses and pass tests similar in range to the étoiles tests of the French ski schools.

In the field of canoeing France and Britain show remarkably similar trends and measures of popularity. Opportunities for mountaineering are limited at French schools, but the Thursday half-holiday is frequently devoted to canoeing and canoe instruction. Instruction is usually based on the headquarters of the local canoe club. In Switzerland the mountains preoccupy thoughts of recreation, and although the country has many excellent canoeing rivers these are overshadowed by the almost magnetic attractions generated by the mountains. With the likely inclusion of canoeing as an EPGS option there is some indication that the sport will increase in popularity. A steady state of popularity for canoeing has been established in Belgium since the middle 1950s. Few additional inducements are offered to school children, and in spite of a scheme of certificates which is largely borrowed from the British Canoe Union, there does not appear to be any great upsurge of interest.

Just as skiing is very clearly the most popular of the mountain activities, it is equally clear that caving is the least popular. This lack of popularity does not, however, invalidate some of the significant differences between the different countries which further serve to underline the essentially different approaches to the educational significance of outdoor pursuits. In each country there has been an increase in participation since the end of the war; this has been most marked in the case of Britain and least in Switzerland.

The Swiss regard the exploration and study of caves more as a science than as a sport and, in spite of many long and interesting systems, there are only some eight hundred cavers in the whole country. It is tempting to argue that with mountain scenery as magnificent as that of Switzerland, there can be little incentive to explore the Stygian gloom of underground passages. Further weight can be added to this argument by relating the degree of popularity of caving to the measure of industrialization and consequent urbanization. In the countries under examination the popularity of caving is proportional to the degree of industrialization. This is clearly seen in Fig. 19, which shows the order of popularity in Belgium, Britain, France and Switzerland.

France, Belgium and Britain have recently introduced qualifications in caving. In Belgium the scheme is similar to that of other outdoor pursuits, with proficiency certificates leading to a hierarchical range of instructors' qualifications. It is tempting to suggest that central administration of a sport makes it far simpler to legislate for training and certification than in a decentralized system which relies on the voluntary co-operation of a number of sporting bodies, whose aims and ideals may be different if not exactly opposed.

OUTDOOR EDUCATION

A survey of the provision for outdoor education in Europe leads to the following basic conclusions:

1. Without exception all the outdoor pursuits are continuing to grow in popularity, and there is every indication that this trend is likely to continue to accelerate in many countries.
2. The popularity of the individual pursuits and the range of studies is dependent on the proximity of amenities and on the degree of both financial and social encouragement which is afforded to them.
3. If the popularity continues to increase, it is likely that a point of saturation of the available resources will be reached. It is not possible to predict a likely date for such an occurrence since, as saturation is approached, the character and pattern of recreation in the countryside are likely to change.
4. Centralized control of sport with its attendant legislation makes for a more coherent pattern of qualifications and for stricter control of instructors and a consequently greater measure of professionalism.
5. Decentralized control of sport can provide appropriate qualifications only where an established need exists and cannot anticipate this need. A proliferation of duplicated certificates can easily result from a lack of control.
6. A general trend towards decentralization of education provides opportunities for experiment, in particular the chance to develop outdoor education programmes, but at the same time makes the provision of a coherent national policy more difficult.
7. The increasing measure of international exchange and co-operation is leading towards a greater measure of awareness of problems and potential, and is providing a basis for the acceptance of a core of content, requirements and standards.
8. Inherent national traits will inevitably continue to colour attitudes towards such aspects as recreation and conservation.
9. Traditional subject boundaries although formerly entrenched show some signs of bending to accommodate the more flexible requirements of an outdoor education programme. This feature is most apparent in the primary schools, but the secondary schools continue to compartmentalize environmental studies and to allow outdoor pursuits a minor role.
10. The full and responsible approach to the introduction and training of young people by the specialist clubs and youth

organizations is greater than in Britain, and may explain the lack of widespread direct promotion in outdoor pursuits particularly in the schools.

Although these trends have a general application to Britain, it is important to underline the main fundamental distinction in the British provision, namely a conscious attempt to integrate the work of environmental education with that of outdoor pursuits. Other countries have perhaps developed their environmental work more conscientiously, but none has achieved the success of the British educational system in encouraging so many young people to participate in outdoor pursuits. It is the combination of environmental work with outdoor pursuits that makes Britain's contribution unique. This contribution, like so many educational innovations, has come about almost by accident, but we should now recognize the fact, and through becoming aware of the particular problems involved make every attempt to overcome them and harness the great appeal which this form of education possesses. In this way Britain can continue to make a unique educational contribution. The safety of increasing numbers of young people can be guarded and the scenic heritage of Britain, which risks irreparable damage, will not only be preserved but will be more fully appreciated by future generations.

Chapter Five

BIBLIOGRAPHY

BURTON T. L. & WIBBERLEY L. *Outdoor Recreation in the British Countryside.* Wye College, 1965.

DANIELS A. S. *Sport and Human Relationships.* International Council of Physical Education, 1964.

DIXON W. *Schools Society and Progress in Scandinavia.* Pergamon Press, 1965.

GRANT N. *Soviet Education.* Penguin Books, 1964.

GREEN F. C. *Jean-Jacques Rousseau—a critical study of his life and writings.* Cambridge University Press, 1955.

KING E. *Communist Education.* Methuen, 1963.

KING E. *Other Schools and Ours.* Holt, Reinhart and Winston, 1966.

MELDRUM K. I. *Mountain Activity Instructors' Certification.* M.Phil. Thesis. Nottingham University, 1970.

PARNOWSKI Z. *Education in Poland.* Polonia Publishing House, Warsaw, 1958.

SAMUEL R. H. *Education and Society in Modern Germany.* Routledge & Kegan Paul, 1949.

SHAPOVALENKO S. G. *Polytechnic Education in the USSR.* UNESCO, 1963.

THUT & ADAMS. *Educational Patterns in Contemporary Society.* McGraw Hill, 1964.

Education in Europe: National Association of Schoolteachers.

Physical Education in Sport. Council for Cultural Co-operation —Strasbourg, 1964.

The Study of the Environment in Schools. UNESCO, 1968.

Final Report of the International working meeting on Environmental Education in school curricula. UCN Morges, Switzerland, 1970.

BELGIUM

MALLINSON V. *Power and Politics in Belgian Education.* Heinemann, 1963.

FRANCE

DUMAZEDIER J. *Towards a Society of Leisure.* The Free Press, Paris, 1962.

FRASER W. R. *Education and Society in Modern France.* Routledge & Kegan Paul, 1963.

HALLS W. D. *Society, Schools and Progress in France.* Pergamon Press, 1963.

THABAULT R. Professional Training in France. *World Year Book of Education*, Evans. 1965.

SWITZERLAND

DOTTRENS R. The Training of Teachers in Switzerland. *World Year Book of Education*. Evans, 1963.

KERR A. *Schools of Europe*. Bowes & Bowes, 1969.

MORANT R. L. *Special Educational Subjects*. 3, HMSO, 1898.

OECHSLI A. *History of Switzerland*. Cambridge University Press, 1922.

RICHOVER H. *Swiss Schools and Ours*. Little Brown & Co, 1962.

AMERICA

GARRISON C. *Outdoor Education. Principles and Practice*. C. C. Thomas, 1966.

JENSEN C. R. *Outdoor Recreation in America. Trends and Problems and Opportunities*. Burgess, 1970.

SMITH J. W. *Outdoor Education*. Prentice Hall, 1963.

SWAN D. M. *Tips and Tricks in Outdoor Education*. Danville Illinois Interstate Printers and Publishers, 1970.

TRUXAL A. G. *Outdoor Recreation Legislation and its Effectiveness*. Columbia University Press, 1929.

Chapter Six
The future

For those who can see the potential of outdoor education, progress is slow and often frustrating. It is of course essential to keep a sense of perspective, but we would maintain that there are not many educational areas which utilize a medium as a tool and have the opportunity to repay the debt so effectively by contributing to the proper use of the environment.

There are, as we hope we have shown, many facets to outdoor education, and although we have concentrated on the practical elements of outdoor pursuits and environmental studies, there are those aspects of social development, creative activity, aesthetic appreciation and stimulating experience which can pervade all that is done and which can be categorized as 'education'. In return it should be possible for this kind of education to influence people's attitudes to both their leisure time and their use and care of natural resources, both issues of personal and national importance. We are convinced that outdoor education has a role to play in the education of young people, and thus in the community as a whole. It is these beliefs, coupled with our own experience and the knowledge of others working in the field, which allow us to look into the future.

Throughout the book we have made a deliberate attempt to look at outdoor education in the light of national developments, the work of appropriate agencies and national bodies, and other school subject areas. First and foremost it is this sort of linked development which we feel should be encouraged in the future. Without being unduly pessimistic there is ample evidence to suggest that we need to be concerned about the relevance of young people's education, especially in the light of the raising of the school leaving age, the opportunities for leisure, the resources for active recreation and the way in which people choose to spend their free time. All of these will increase the already large numbers of people using parts of the countryside, and especially areas of particular attraction.

Clearly outdoor education cannot solve these problems, nor is it the only agency which could claim to have any relevance in attempting to solve them. However, we would claim that it has a contribution to make in conjunction with the other bodies or agencies equally concerned. There is no doubt that in these issues the national bodies have a large part to play. There are signs that they are prepared to, but it is still the case that they align themselves with a specific area and do not link with or encroach on other domains.

There needs to be, in our opinion, much greater co-ordination between the work of the Countryside Commission and the Sports Council. At the moment one is dealing principally with the countryside as a natural resource and protecting it, and the other with the established games and sports. Active recreation in the countryside or on the water appears to drop between the two stools. It may be that there is something to commend the pattern which has emerged in so many sports, the development of schools associations connected to the senior body, e.g. the British Schools Canoeing Association and the British Canoe Union, and to bodies such as the Countryside Commission or the National Trust. In this way the requirements of both education and young people in general could be more easily reflected in policy and practice. At the moment only the Royal Society for the Protection of Birds, as a national body involved in aspects of the countryside, has seen the significance of this sort of approach.

The problems of accommodating young people in adult organizations was touched on in chapter four. In the future the specialist adult clubs and societies will need to accept the responsibility for bridging the gap between leaving school and joining an adult group as a full member. Such groups should be encouraged to accept this responsibility through a system of promotion and grants from the Countryside Commission, sports councils and departments of education. Financial help and appropriate training

153

courses should be made more readily available for potential leaders. They in turn could develop junior sections of their own organizations and through subsidized training courses. Such a scheme is employed with great success in Switzerland and has the advantage of providing the clubs and societies with a steady source of new members and at the same time of integrating young people into a responsible adult society.

The formation of the Select Committee of the House of Lords on Sport and Leisure is an indication that developments along the lines suggested are, not surprisingly, in other people's minds.

The brief of the Committee is: 'To consider the demand for facilities for participation in sport and in the enjoyment of leisure out-of-doors and to examine what impediments may exist to the fuller use of existing facilities or the development of new ones and how they might be removed.'

We have mentioned that co-ordination of all those bodies involved at national level is essential, and that a balanced rather than a specific or even specialist approach should prevail when appropriate. This same attitude is one which needs to be encouraged between people requiring the same environment for varied purposes.

There are few signs that the traditional and persistent incompatibilities of certain recreations can be solved without a fuller appreciation of each other's requirements and problems, and without some element of sacrifice or destruction. Classic examples of such attitudes are given by the bitter controversies existing between the owners of shooting estates and hill walkers; angling interests and canoeists; conservationists and developers; natural resources and contrived amenities.

Restrictive control imposed by national agencies and local bodies will only serve to exacerbate the existing problems; co-operation and understanding developed through education and information are more likely to achieve the aim of peaceful co-existence.

It seems likely that centres such as Landmark in the Cairngorms, Brockhole in the Lake District and the National Trust for Scotland's centre at Ben Lawers will be the information centres of the future. It seems strange that at the moment although many people going into the countryside find their contribution interesting and helpful it would appear that mountaineers, canoeists, sailors and cavers would not favour similar centres say in Snowdonia, on the Spey or south coast, or in the Yorkshire Dales designed and equipped to increase their knowledge, information and awareness.

Advocating co-operation between the influential organizations, and between the individual interests involved in using the country-side, suggesting much closer and more detailed involvement at all levels by those involved in education, and by those being sub-jected to both the educational and the national patterns, and suggesting that conflict between the two aspects might well be lessened by learning from each other, provides the first group of developments for the future.

It is not the function of this book, and it is beyond our com-petence, to look closely at the policies and practices of public and private bodies in relation to outdoor education. Our main concern as we have stressed throughout is with education. At the outset we attempted to outline the ways in which the two major components of outdoor education, outdoor pursuits and countryside studies, were being used by those working in the educational field, and drew the conclusion that it could number amongst the valuable aids the broad education of all pupils.

It will be necessary in the future for the role and content of out-door education to be examined constantly. It is difficult to define precisely the range over which outdoor education can and should spread. Certainly to give the impression that it is all embracing would be misleading and confusing. Art and physical education teachers, geographers, biologists, amongst many others, have used the 'outdoors' as an additional dimension to their own subjects, and this is a situation which will inevitably continue and even be extended. However, it is our belief that it is possible to produce a distinctive core to outdoor education based on exploration, inquiry and understanding centred around outdoor pursuits and environ-mental studies, which at the thematic level would be appropriate for all pupils and which would create a foundation from which deeper studies and skill-learning could take place.

It is interesting to discover that many teachers and organizations involved in outdoor pursuits or environmental studies, but working independently, had similar aims. Summarized they were as follows:

1. The learning of a new outdoor skill or the strengthening of an existing interest or skill.

155

2. The ability to work as a team, mix happily and yet allow for individuality.
3. Enjoyment of the countryside and appreciation of its beauty.
4. An appreciation through awareness and understanding of the natural environment; its problems and potential for leisure, conservation, economic and human use.
5. The possibilities for individual development through informal discussions, projects and other cultural, intellectual and physical pursuits.
6. Out of the classroom evidence that the pupils found practical work more pleasurable and that they became more interested, more co-operative and that they worked harder, and that this sort of work had a considerable effect on relationships and subsequent work in school.

From these factors, and of course those others also mentioned, particularly in chapter one, allied to the practical skills and features of outdoor pursuits and environmental studies, we feel that there is a great deal to commend outdoor education as a contributor to non-specialist learning in the early years of secondary school, leading to both structured opportunities and informed choice of interests and other subjects in the fourth, fifth and sixth years.

Definition

Outdoor education is a means of approaching educational objectives through guided, direct experience in the environment, using its resources as learning materials. The theme should be one of 'exploration and inquiry' at foundation level, leading to progressive, new and lasting skills, interests and learning.

Content

Creative Activities. Here the aim should be to use the environment to stimulate original work and thought, particularly drawing on dimensions of art, drama, photography and crafts.

Environmental Studies. The aim should be to create a better understanding and appreciation of both the potential and the

156

problems of the environment, and to use such areas as forests, the coast and open countryside for specific study and general observation.

Outdoor Pursuits. The aim should be to involve young people in mentally and physically stimulating pursuits: mountaineering, skiing, sailing, canoeing, pony trekking, orienteering, sub-aqua and expeditions. Any of these may lead them into adopting new interests and create fresh enthusiasms. Such skills will enable them to examine, and hopefully understand, fresh and exciting environments in safety and relative comfort, and at the same time provide inspiration for original creative work.

Social Aspects. The aim should be to offer situations where the participants are dependent on each other and learn to acknowledge this, and at the same time develop self-confidence to cope with practical and intellectual situations which can be created. Residential experience at a centre, hostel or camp, coupled with an activity, study or pursuits, is of considerable value in this field. It is desirable that links are forged between a variety of subject disciplines and other educational areas, and it is this synthesis which enables the production of lasting values and opportunities and outdoor education.

We therefore see the necessity for a clear definition and a thoroughly organized place in the education of all pupils for outdoor education. We hope that this book assists in the preparation of the former, and that we have not avoided outlining the practical requirements of such a policy.

We have given in chapter three details of existing school pro-programmes which are both properly organized and imaginative. There are other examples which we could not include, but which we recognize.

However, it is our opinion that at the moment there are few education authority or school programmes which direct the attention towards an acceptable pattern for the introduction and development of outdoor education, and which do not rely on these being largely a matter of chance rather than design, and on voluntary work by teachers rather than through a structured system.

The greatest need, apart from the recognition of outdoor education as a contributor to education and the community, is for the emergence of training courses for prospective teachers. It is our opinion that outdoor education should be conducted in the schools by fully trained and experienced teachers. We recognize the very real problems in training specialist teachers in outdoor education to work in schools. Such posts may only serve to compartmentalize yet another school subject. We have tried to show throughout the book that outdoor education is more a philosophical attitude towards education as a whole than just a mixture of the most exciting aspects culled from the traditional range of school subjects. It is a philosophy which can pervade all subjects, and consequently all teachers should at least be aware of the difficulties and opportunities which a comprehensive outdoor education programme may create. Through an appreciation of these they might be more sympathetic to the ideals involved. Perhaps the principal aim of an outdoor education specialist in the school context should be that of innovator and co-ordinator through whose enthusiasm the outdoor education programme both within the school time-table and out of school hours can be implemented. If the colleges of education are to undertake the training of teachers of outdoor education in an increasingly professional way both through pre-service and in-service courses it is essential that the schools should be able to provide the necessary openings for these teachers, and that they should lead to a clearly defined career structure.

There are of course other requirements, and we can do no better than reproduce the recommendations made in a National Association for Outdoor Education circular (March 1972), which points out the unsatisfactory and possibly unsafe practice of encouraging programmes of outdoor education without providing the essential prerequisites, namely:

1. There should be a reappraisal of leadership training and qualification schemes operated by the national bodies.
2. There is an urgent need for the training of teachers and leaders of outdoor education at main subject level in universities and colleges of education.
3. In-service training courses should be increased and support given to those wishing to attend them.
4. Support be given to research into the physical and psychological limitations of adolescents in demanding outdoor situations.
5. The provision of staff and resources should be reviewed in

order that outdoor education can be conducted in a safe and progressive manner.

6. An examination should be made of the career structure, conditions of service and responsibilities of those involved in outdoor education, and particularly in outdoor pursuits.

7. There should be an overall and cohesive structure for all aspects of outdoor education within local authorities and voluntary organizations.

Without doubt there is a growing awareness of the value of outdoor education as one means of educating young people whether it be for physical, social, mental or aesthetic ends and of the paradoxical situation of not having properly trained teachers or adequate resources.

It would be interesting to know how many teachers conducting programmes have access to an annual share of the schools' *per capita* allowance and how many have to take what is left, utilize a hand-out from the physical education department for tents or from the geography department for maps, or even deplete the sum set aside for the library simply by being persistent. Few schools to our knowledge have an equipment room or adequate storage space, let alone a planning or project area always available. Often transport facilities are inadequate, and there is usually little money available to subsidize school camps, visits or foreign travel. There is no one to blame for this situation—it has simply evolved and been largely accepted by education departments, head teachers and teachers alike. It would be fair to point out that many teachers would resent a structured approach and easily obtained resources on the grounds that a great deal of the value of this sort of work has been because of the voluntary effort and the slow accumulation of time, equipment, transport and money.

In the future this could probably continue, and whilst we favour the production of imaginative programmes produced out of conviction, we feel that these can be achieved with rather more ease and with much wider effect through the provision of adequate and appropriate resources.

At this point it is logical to look towards the future of the established centres. Whilst recognizing their pioneering role, their value and the problems they have had to face, we see their future in providing courses which fit the needs of the pupils. Many outdoor

159

pursuits centres have concentrated too much on physical skills and many field study centres on scientific skills. This imbalance needs to be reconsidered.

The expected growth of programmes in schools and the provision of day resource centres for outdoor education should enable the residential centres to fulfil their role, when required, of providing specialist courses and teaching, and it is for this that many of them are equipped at the moment—but in only one or two aspects of outdoor education and often in isolation of the pupils' previous or continuing experiences.

We are aware of the criticism which is being levelled at comprehensive outdoor education programmes by national agencies connected with field studies and outdoor recreation, in particular the accusation that by introducing large numbers of young people to specialist activities outdoor education is in danger of flooding Britain's limited resources. Although we deplore the concept of legislative restrictions, it is quite clear that the growth in popularity of both outdoor pursuits and countryside studies may mean that some controls will ultimately become desirable.

The very numbers involved are likely to change the character of all countryside activities to such an extent that they become unrecognizable. For example, the extensive defences at the Boat of Garten osprey nesting site with the organized observation towers inevitably destroy much of the spontaneity of the experience, and render it more akin to a visit to an aviary. Again, mountaineering, whose principal attraction lay in the opportunities it presented to escape to isolated regions, now, because of the large numbers involved, has become essentially a gregarious pastime where the concept of queueing for climbs is in no way foreign.

Just as it would be invidious for us to deplore such changes, and to imply that today's climbers and ornithologists derive less pleasure from their pastime than their predecessors, so it would be wrong for us to deny the possibility that restrictions, although changing the character of countryside activities, would of necessity render them less beneficial or less enjoyable. Artificially contrived facilities and simulated situations tend to promote interest in countryside activity at the moment. Examples of these are plastic ski slopes, artificial climbing walls, concrete canoe slalom courses, electronic equipment for simulated sailing, and conceivably nature trails and planned camp sites. In the future such provisions, along with the techniques of access control through geographical and time zoning, charges and denial, may act as substitutes for or constraints on the over-use and destruction of natural facilities and habitats.

Though there needs to be very careful consideration given to introducing large numbers of pupils to the countryside it is our belief that through education the problem may be anticipated and met constructively rather than accentuated.

It will be gathered from this chapter that we see the necessity for:

1. National bodies to become more closely aligned and involved in the requirements of young people at school and in the years immediately after leaving.
2. Clubs and societies to play a full role in the continuing development of young people's interests.
3. A greater co-operation between users of the countryside in order to solve access and joint use problems.
4. The creation of more resources to increase understanding of all users of the countryside.
5. Education directed in such a way that there will not be the pressing necessity to impose direct controls and restrictions on the use of natural resources.

In the educational area we would once again refer to the recommendations of the National Association for Outdoor Education and stress the need for:

1. The development of outdoor education as an accepted part of every pupil's education.
2. The full potential of outdoor education to be widely recognized.
3. The development of outdoor education to be subject to continuing review.
4. The integration of it with other subject areas to avoid the wasteful effect of duplication or saturation, and to make it pupil centred rather than subject orientated.
5. The absolute necessity of having properly trained teachers in schools and centres.
6. The creation of a proper organization in schools to develop and organize programmes of work.

7. Ample resources to conduct programmes progressively and safely.

Whilst ourselves not considering these suggestions at all revolutionary, we are not unaware of the implications of cost, time, effort and reorganization which will be required. Cause for revolution enough.

Appendix A

British Canoe Union,
26–9 Park Crescent,
London W1

British Orienteering Federation,
3 Glenfinlas Street,
Edinburgh

British Schools Exploring
  Society,
2 Whitehall Court,
London SW1

British Trust for Ornithology,
Beech Grove,
Tring,
Hertfordshire

British Waterways,
Melbury House,
Melbury Terrace,
London NW1

Conservation Society,
21 Hanyards Lane,
Cuffley,
Potters Bar,
Hertfordshire

Committee on Education and
  the Countryside,
St Andrews House,
Edinburgh

Council for Environmental
  Education,
26 Bedford Square,
London WC1

Council for Nature,
Zoological Gardens,
Regent's Park,
London NW1

Duke of Edinburgh Award
  Scheme,
2 Old Queen Street,
London W1

Field Studies Council,
9 Devereux Court,
Strand,
London WC2

Geographical Association,
343 Fulwood Road,
Sheffield 10

Girl Guides Association,
17–19 Buckingham Palace Road,
London SW1

International Youth Federation
  for Environmental Studies
  and Conservation,
c/o IUCN,
1110 Morges,
Switzerland

Mountain Leadership Training
  Boards,
The Sports Councils,
26 Park Crescent,
London W1

and 4 Queensferry Street,
Edinburgh

163

National Association for
Outdoor Education,
Buckden House,
Buckden,
Skipton,
Yorkshire

National Rural and Environ-
mental Studies Association,
Offley Place,
Great Offley,
Near Hitchin,
Hertfordshire

National Schools Sailing
Association,
Educational Offices,
County Hall,
Chichester

National Ski Federation,
118 Eaton Square,
London SW1

Nature Conservancy,
19 Belgrave Square,
London SW1

and 5 Hope Terrace,
Edinburgh

Outward Bound Trust,
73 Great Peter Street,
London SW1

Physical Education Association,
Ling House,
10 Nottingham Place,
London W1

Ramblers Association,
124 Finchley Road,
London NW3

Royal Society for Protection of
Birds *and* Young Ornitholo-
gists Club,
The Lodge,
Sandy,
Bedfordshire

Royal Society for the Prevention
of Accidents,
Terminal House,
52 Grosvenor Gardens,
London SW1

Schools Council,
60 Great Portland Street,
London W1N 6LL

Scottish National Ski Council,
The Barn,
Balmore,
Torrance,
Near Glasgow

The Conservation Corps,
Zoological Gardens,
Regents Park,
London NW1

The Countryside Commission,
1 Cambridge Gate,
Regents Park,
London NW1 4JJ

and Battleby,
Redgorton,
Perth

The National Trusts,
42 Queen Anne's Gate,
London SW1

and 5 Charlotte Square,
Edinburgh

The Scout Association,
25 Buckingham Palace Road,
London SW1

The Society for the Promotion
  of Nature Reserves,
The Manor House,
Alford,
Lincolnshire

Society for Environmental
  Education,
16 Trinity Road,
Elderby,
Leicestershire

Town and Country Planning
  Association,
17 Carlton House Terrace,
London SW1Y 5AS

Wildlife Youth Service,
Wallington,
Surrey

World Wildlife Fund,
7–8 Plumtree Court,
London EC4

Youth Hostel Association,
Trevelyan House,
St Albans,
Hertfordshire

Appendix B

This certificate is the minimum qualification which is acceptable by most authorities for the leadership of groups in mountain environments during summer conditions. The certificate is administered by the Mountain Leadership Training Boards (26 Park Crescent, London W1, and 4 Queensferry Street, Edinburgh EH2 4PB) who can provide full details. The syllabus to be covered before a one-week assessment course is as follows:

Map and compass

Map scales.
Conventional signs.
Map references—the grid.
Methods of showing relief.
Contours—description of ground from information on the map.
Topographical features.
Measurement of distance.
Calculation of speed of movement over varying terrain with and without loads—Naismith's rule.
Setting of the map—without compass.
Navigation across country with map but no compass.
Types of compass.
Methods of obtaining grid and magnetic bearings.
Plotting a compass course from the ground and from the map.
Method of obtaining a position fix by resection (back-bearing).
Navigation across country with map and compass, especially in poor visibility (e.g. at night).
Hints on natural wayfinding (e.g. use of sun or stars).
Methods of teaching simple map and compass work for beginners.

Route planning

Choice of route.
Preparation of route cards:
(*a*) Bearings.

166

(*b*) Distances covered.
(*c*) Time taken.
Selection of camp sites.
Expedition rationing.
Escape routes.
Bad weather alternatives.
Sources of aid (telephones, M.R. posts, etc.).

Walking skills

Individual skills—pace, rhythm, foot placing, conservation of energy, balance and co-ordination.
Party skills—leader and tailman, psychology of the group, corporate strength.
Party procedure on different terrain, e.g. scree, narrow ridge, steep broken slopes.

Personal equipment

Personal equipment required for mountain expeditions, both high and low level and in all weather conditions. Information given should stress the effects of wind, temperature and humidity as well as providing information on design construction and types of material, care and maintenance of equipment.

Camping equipment

Knowledge of the use of different types and makes of :
(*a*) Tents.
(*b*) Sleeping-bags.
(*c*) Stoves.
(*d*) Rucksacks and other lightweight camping equipment.
Knowledge of the principles of packing and loading personal and communal equipment.
Care and maintenance of camping equipment.
Knowledge of items required on given types of expedition, e.g. high level/low level, long duration/short duration camps.

Campcraft

Camp organization and siting.
Tent organization and siting.
Camp daily routine.
Hygiene on camp.
The country code.
Camp foods and cooking.
Use of mountain huts and bothies.

Security on steep ground

The small amount of rock climbing included in the course is not
intended to train leaders as rock climbers. Its purpose is to
familiarize candidates with elementary techniques, to enable them
to appreciate the limits of what should be attempted by a party
without rock climbing experience, to recognize difficulties and
potential dangers of terrain and to give competent help in cases of
emergency. Any safe method of rope management will be accepted
at assessment, but the method used and taught should involve the
use of the rope alone. It is emphasized that the techniques here are
not necessarily those which would be suitable for rock climbing.
The following points will be dealt with:

(*a*) Practice of movement on rock.
(*b*) Ropes and rope management. Tying-on—figure of eight on the
    bight; waist belay with gloves; belaying and interchange of
    belay; moving together.
(*c*) Decision taking on steep, broken ground. Route selection,
    roping up, choice of belay, negotiating loose rock, etc.
(*d*) Use and limitations of hill walking safety line (120′ of No. 2
    laid rope or 7-mm or 9-mm Kernmantel rope).
(*e*) Use of rope as a handrail and for linking party together.
(*f*) Abseiling with safety rope.

River crossing

When and when not to ford rivers followed by practice in:

(*a*) Methods of finding the best crossing points.
(*b*) Methods of crossing with and without line.
(*c*) Skills and safety precautions to be practised by the individual

168

method of progression, use of 'third leg', procedure with a pack, reduction of resistance or friction, danger from trees and snags.

Special mountain hazards

Exposure. An understanding of the causes of the condition known as 'exposure' or 'hypothermia'. Recognition of the signs and symptoms exhibited by 'exposure' cases. Awareness of the basis for prevention of 'exposure'. Awareness of the methods for treatment of an 'exposure' case:

(*a*) in the field, and
(*b*) at base.

Frostbite. An understanding of the condition, its signs, symptoms, prevention and treatment.

Lightning. An understanding of the probable distribution of strikes on a mountain, and of the probable flow lines of resulting ground currents.

Heat exhaustion. An understanding of the condition, its signs and symptoms, prevention and treatment.

Weather

An elementary knowledge of weather, e.g.:
Interpretation of the weather map recognizing:
  (*a*) Areas of high pressure.
  (*b*) Air flows (e.g. northerly airstream).
  (*c*) Depressions and frontal systems, and weather normally associated with these.
Major cloud forms and associated weather developments.
Sources of information on weather, e.g. newspapers, radio/television broadcasts, RAF stations.

Accident procedure

Candidates must have practical ability and theoretical knowledge in depth of the following:
(*a*) Procedure in the event of an accident.

(*b*) Methods of search and evacuation.
(*c*) Equipment contained in M.R. posts and boxes.
(*d*) Improvised mountain equipment—application and limitations.
  rope seats
  rope stretchers
  sleds
  ski stretchers

Details of clubs, organizations, etc.

Details of organizations providing training in mountain activities.
Details of clubs, etc., willing to accept young people as members.
Guide books, etc.

Responsibilities of party leader, etc.

A thorough knowledge and awareness of the function and responsibilities of the party leader.

Additional interests

A mountain leader should be knowledgeable about some or all of the following subjects: geology, flora and fauna, local history, history of mountaineering, photography, etc.

First Aid

An adult first aid certificate must be obtained.

Appendix C

This certificate is the minimum acceptable qualification for teachers taking groups into mountain environments in winter conditions. It is a supplementary certificate to the summer Mountain Leadership Certificate, the holding of which is a prerequisite for assessment. This certificate is administered by the Scottish Mountain Leadership Board (4 Queensferry Street, Edinburgh EH2 4PB). Details of the syllabus and method of assessment are as follows.

Syllabus

For assessment purposes, candidates will be required to be familiar with the theory and practice of the following:

Carrying the ice axe.

Kicking steps up and down in snow.

Use of the axe; walking, step cutting up and down, belaying, glissading, probing.

Braking, in self-arrest technique.

Holding a fall on steep snow from above and from below.

Step cutting on ice, with and without crampons.

Cramponing up, and down, and traversing.

Belaying on ice—use of pitons and screws.

Surmounting a cornice.

Moving together.

Winter climbing at Grade I standard.

Special equipment (individual and group) necessary for winter mountaineering.

Winter campcraft.

Construction of snow holes and emergency shelters.

Knowledge of the causes, symptoms and treatment of exposure and frostbite.

A knowledge of the development of weather systems in winter time.

A basic knowledge of the process of firnification and evaluation of avalanche risk.

Winter search and evacuation techniques, including the searching of avalanche tips.

A sound knowledge of the planning of winter expeditions and the special responsibilities of the party leader.

Exemptions

Experienced mountaineers may elect, in the light of their experience, to exempt themselves from training courses and proceed direct to assessment but must be in possession of a current adult certificate in first aid, together with awfully completed log book; both documents to be presented to the director of assessment.

Assessment

Candidates will be assessed on the basis of their ability to lead others in winter conditions as well as their personal competence in the various skills.

The Board will appoint a director of assessment to whom shall be delegated the responsibility for making all necessary arrangements.

Subsequent to assessment of candidates, the director of assessment will make recommendations to the Board regarding the award of certificates.

Appendix D

Mountaineering Instructor's Certificate

This certificate is the minimum qualification for all round mountaineering, including rock climbing. It is administered by the Mountain Leadership Training Boards. The syllabus is as follows:

Before being accepted for assessment each candidate should usually have completed a one-week's training course or the equivalent. In addition, he must have satisfied his tutors as regards the following:

1. Substantial experience in at least three mountain districts, e.g. North Wales, Lake District, Skye.
2. At least twelve hill walking expeditions involving mobile camps or bivouacs, half to have been in the winter months of December to March.
3. Three years' rock climbing experience and have led twenty-five very difficult or higher rock climbs, on big cliffs such as Lliwedd, Pillar, Buachaille. (These climbs must be listed with dates.) A candidate should be able to lead unseen and in poor weather any climb of this standard.
4. A minimum of six weeks (forty-two days) as instructor in mountain craft on courses recognized by the Board—e.g. at Wardens' Association Centres, or special LEA and Sports Council courses.
5. Possession of the Scottish Mountain Leadership Winter Certificate.
6. Possession of a valid Adult First Aid Certificate.

Syllabus

Candidates will be assessed at a one-week assessment on their knowledge of the syllabus given below.

Complete familiarity with the syllabus material will be expected. Candidates must be able to speak fluently about all aspects of the work and be able to answer questions to a class. They must show an ability to illustrate the syllabus material from personal experience and to approach difficult areas of teaching in a variety of ways.

173

Candidates are recommended to become fully conversant with the material presented in *Mountain Leadership*, the official handbook of the Mountain Leadership Boards of Great Britain.

Candidates must be able to undertake difficult and strenuous mountain journeys, and demonstrate with the ease of long practice the art of navigation in mountains. The highest standards of campcraft and bivouac techniques will be demanded, and the candidate's ability to achieve comfort in the wildest of situations will be noted.

1. *Map and compass work: theory and practical*

Map references.

Map scales.

Conventional signs.

Topographical features.

Setting of map with and without the use of compass.

Measurement of distance and calculations of speed of movement on varying terrain—with and without loads.

Methods of showing relief. Contours of glaciated country, sections, gradients, intervisibility. The limitations of contours. Reading ground from information on a map.

Compass—types of compass and methods of obtaining grid and magnetic bearings. Plotting of courses.

Practice in cross-country navigation with a map and without a compass.

Practice in navigation with a compass at night and in whiteout conditions.

Methods of resection and obtaining position by resection.

Hints on natural way-finding, e.g. use of sun and stars.

The National Grid—its false origin, primary squares and their subdivisions. The difference between grid and true north.

Organization and control of map and compass exercises and orienteering courses.

Knowledge of continental maps.

Knowledge of place names.

A simple explanation of how maps are made and of the earth's magnetic field is often asked for by students, therefore background reading in these areas is important to an instructor.

2. *Route planning*

Choice of route, preparation of route card and choice of 'escape' routes or bad weather alternatives.

3. *Walking skills*

Refer to *Safety on Mountains*.

Individual skills—pace, rhythm, conservation of energy, foot placing, balance and co-ordination.

Procedure of party when scrambling or on rough terrain, e.g. scree, narrow ridges and steep broken slopes.

4. *Personal equipment*

Personal equipment required for mountain and moorland expeditions in *all* weather conditions. Information given should stress the effects of wind, temperature and humidity, as well as providing information on design, construction and types of material to look for. Care of equipment and emphasis on personal and group selection of equipment, bearing in mind factors such as cost and durability.

5. *Camping equipment*

Examination of equipment and demonstration of use, i.e. stove lighting, load carrying and packing, tents and tent erection.

Other camp equipment and advice on suitability and care of equipment. Emphasis on personal and group selection of equipment, bearing in mind factors such as cost and durability.

6. *Camp craft and bivouaccing : Camp planning*

Refer to *Expedition Guide*.

Organization of the whole camp and individual tents.

Choice of site and siting of tents.

Camp foods—cooking and planning of meals.

Use of mountain huts and bothies.

Hygiene in huts, bothies and on camps.

Knowledge of the Country Code.

Use of emergency bivouacs.

175

7. *Expedition planning*

Have an understanding of the relevant issues required for the care of young people in the mountains, particularly load carrying capacity and long distance capability of individuals and the maintenance of morale.

Ability to plan a mobile expedition in a remote mountain area.

Knowledge of requirements of the expedition section of the Duke of Edinburgh Award.

Ability to plan and control a number of groups, moving independently, such as on Duke of Edinburgh Award Gold Expeditions, so that a right balance between adventure and safety is maintained.

Relation of routes to conditions, weather, terrain, time of the year, group size, age, sex, fitness and suitability of group's equipment.

8. *Weather*

Knowledge of air masses and their properties with particular reference to the four main types affecting the British Isles, generally as airstreams.

- (*a*) maritime polar   mP
- (*b*) continental polar   cP
- (*c*) maritime tropical   mT
- (*d*) continental tropical   cT

Knowledge of weather associated with anti-cyclones, depressions and frontal systems (summer and winter).

Ability to infer local situations from information given on BBC sound and television programmes, including the BBC shipping forecasts (1500 metres long wave-length service).

Ability to read a synoptic chart as shown in some national newspapers or on television, and to infer local situations from the information given.

Knowledge of main cloud types and awareness of significant signs indicating weather changes.

Knowledge of the significance of barometric pressure and changes in wind direction and in humidity.

Knowledge of the effect of altitude and of landforms on weather conditions.

Knowledge of the occurrence and significance of micro-climate.

Knowledge of the Beaufort scale, including the symbols used on charts, the descriptions, the wind speeds and means of recognition, particularly of Force 6 (i.e. strong breeze) upwards to Force 10 (whole gale).

9. *Rock climbing*

History of rock climbing in Britain—growth of clubs, BMC, outdoor centres, MLTB, etc. Development of techniques and equipment.
Where to climb in Britain—grading of climbs and guide books.
Organizing a series of indoor rock climbing sessions.
Organizing a rock climbing lesson for four to five beginners on a practice rock.
Leading and instructing two more advanced pupils on a large cliff climb of very difficult standard.
Teaching an acceptable rope technique and having a knowledge of various other methods, including artificial climbing. Being familiar with the use and misuse of climbing aids, including slings, pitons, nuts, karabiners, etc.

10. *Scottish mountain leadership winter certificate*

Candidates will be expected to have made every attempt to have gained the Winter Certificate prior to attending for MIC assessment.

11. *River crossings*

When and when not to ford rivers, followed by practice in:
(*a*) Methods of finding the best crossing points.
(*b*) Methods of crossing with and without a line.
(*c*) Skills and safety precautions to be used by the individual, e.g. method of progression, use of a 'third' leg, procedure with a pack, reduction of resistance or friction, danger from trees and snags.

12. *Mountain rescue*

Main causes of mountain accidents.
The distress signals.

Action of party members, e.g. application of simple first aid, the four essentials of information, procedure in exceptional circumstances.

Mountain rescue posts, police assistance, RAF mountain rescue, the first-aid organizations and their function in the rescue service.

Ability to organize a search and evacuation.

Knowledge of visual communications.

Faniliarity with various stretchers, e.g. Thomas, Duff, MacInnes, Mariner and use of a Thomas splint.

Ability to take part in the evacuation of an injured climber from a cliff, using an acceptable method.

Knowledge of other equipment, such as types of illumination for night work, radios, etc.

Mouth to mouth (nose) resuscitation.

Improvisation of rescue equipment.

13. *Responsibilities of party leader*

The skills of party leader should be understood as:

(*a*) Party leader to choose route, set pace, appoint rear man, ensure the adequate equipping of the party and make all necessary decisions leading to the good conduct and safety of the party. Extra equipment to be carried by the leader.

(*b*) Responsibilities of rear man.

14. *Special mountain hazards*

Recognition and treatment of cases of exhaustion and exposure.

Effect of sun and heat.

Effects of lightning.

Recognition and treatment of frostbite.

15. *Law relating to access to land*

Knowledge of the Countryside Acts (Scotland and England) and an understanding of the parts played by such bodies as the Countryside Commission, the National Trust, the Nature Conservancy and the Forestry Commission, etc.

Appendix E

This is the highest professional qualification in mountaineering and the candidate must have:

1. Held the Mountaineering Instructor's Certificate for at least one year, and have gained other relevant experience to the satisfaction of the Boards.

   Attended a residential assessment of one week's duration at one of the national mountain centres, or at a centre approved for this purpose under a director of assessment appointed by the Boards.

2. The candidate is required to demonstrate his ability in all aspects of the MIC syllabus at a higher level.

   He must also:

(a) Be capable of leading and instructing to VS standard on rock and leading artificial climbs at grade A2/A3.

(b) Have at least three seasons' snow and ice climbing experience, and be capable of leading and instructing to Grade II standard, in addition to holding the Scottish Mountain Leadership Winter Certificate.

(c) Be able to organize a large-scale search and evacuation.

(d) Be able to demonstrate ability to organize the evacuation of an injured climber from a major cliff, using acceptable vertical and horizontal lowering methods.

(e) Have a knowledge of the progressive programming of various mountain activities.

(f) Have an understanding of the mountain environment, and in particular of one area.

(g) Have developed one or more specialist studies related to the mountain environment, and produce appropriate evidence of this for assessment purposes.

(h) Have an understanding of the relevant issues required for the care of young people in the mountains.

Appendix F

The canoeing certificates are administered by the British Canoe
Union (26 Park Crescent, London W1) and the Scottish Canoe
Association (4 Queensferry Street, Edinburgh EH2 4PB). The
basic format of the coaching scheme involves two areas, inland
water and sea, and is as follows:

Inland proficiency (kayak)

This is the standard of personal performance required before a
candidate can undertake instructor's training. The course covers
personal safety and safety of equipment, understanding river
features and conditions, and the ability to handle a kayak competently.

Senior instructor (inland kayak)

This award is intended for experienced canoeists who hold the
Inland Proficiency (kayak) Certificate, and who now wish to train
groups of canoeists. Courses include the full syllabus of the Senior
Instructor Award, which stresses the management and safety of
group canoeing and the training of beginners to a high standard of
proficiency. Continuous assessment is made throughout the course
and successful candidates may receive a probationary certificate
entitling them to act as an assistant instructor. This certificate will
be valid for twelve months, and the candidate will be expected to
gain as much instructing experience as possible during this time.
He must then present himself for testing for the Senior Instructor
Award (inland) between the sixth and twelfth month of the
certificate's validity.

Sea proficiency

This is the standard of personal performance required before a
candidate can undertake instructor's training. The course covers

personal safety and safety of equipment, understanding sea conditions and features, tides and effects of wind, the ability to handle the kayak competently at sea and the performance of deep-water rescue.

Senior instructor (sea)

This award is intended for experienced canoeists who hold the Sea Proficiency Certificate and who now wish to train groups of canoeists. The course includes the full syllabus of the Senior Instructor Award, which stresses the management and safety of group canoeing and the training of beginners to a high standard of proficiency. Continuous assessment is made throughout the course and successful candidates may receive a probationary certificate entitling them to act as an assistant instructor. This certificate will be valid for twelve months, and the candidates will be expected to gain as much instructing experience as possible during this time. He must then present himself for testing for the Senior Instructor Award (sea) between the sixth and twelfth months of the certificate's validity.

Advanced Inland Proficiency (kayak)

This is the standard of personal performance required before a candidate can undertake training for the Coaches Award. Candidates must hold the Inland Proficiency (kayak) Certificate. The course covers advanced techniques on white water, rolling, and the planning and leadership of advanced river trips.

Advanced Sea Proficiency

This is the standard of personal performance required before a candidate can undertake training for the Coaches Award. Candidates must hold the Sea Proficiency Certificate. The course covers advanced techniques at sea, rolling, understanding and use of charts, and the planning and leadership of advanced sea trips.

Coaches Awards

This award is intended for those who hold two advanced proficiency certificates, have a wide and throrough knowledge of the sport and who now wish to become involved in the instruction of canoeing at an advanced level. The course will cover the full syllabus of the Coaches Award, which includes the teaching of a group of canoeist's skills to advanced test standards, organization and running of indoor and outdoor courses, practical teaching techniques, design and construction and a detailed look at all types of competition. Continuous assessment will be made throughout the course, and the successful candidate will receive a probationary certificate entitling him to act as assistant coach. This certificate will be valid for twelve months, and during this time the candidate will be expected to gain as much experience as possible. He should then present himself for testing between the sixth and the twelfth month of the certificate's validity.

Appendix G

Ski party leader
Grade III—assistant instructor.
Grade II—ski instructor.
Grade I—ski teacher.

It must be quite clearly understood that these courses are not designed to cater for bringing people's personal skiing ability up to the required level. It is taken for granted that all who apply can ski to a very good parallel standard in most snow conditions. Candidates must progress from Grade III to Grade I, attending all courses, as the content of any one course is only part of the whole syllabus.

The emphasis throughout the syllabus is on the breakdown of the technique, and the method of putting over this breakdown, i.e. the teaching. Confusion and misinterpretation of ski techniques have been caused by translations, the personality cult, improper publicity and promotion, and writers on ski technique who are not qualified. Similarly confusion is caused by experimental theory being used as a new method before being proven. We do not insist on prolonged basic manœuvres as in the old days. The final forms are the goal of the student, and emphasis is put on using natural positions to achieve those ends. The instructor, on the other hand, must be perfect in the demonstration of the finished form. Teaching method will be covered at every opportunity, both during teaching by the trainer and during the candidate's personal skiing and teaching. It is possible that a programme will involve a morning of teaching by the trainer, and an afternoon spent mainly with the candidates teaching in turn those parts of the syllabus chosen by the trainer.

Classes will be made up in the first place from information supplied by the candidate. Where necessary an individual will be moved to a class of his or her ability during the first day.

183

Syllabus for candidates for all grades

Introduction of skis to pupils on snow.
Explaining bindings, operation and introduction of sticks.
Standing exercises.
Walking on the flat.
Step turns, kick turns.
Side stepping, herring-bone.
Straight running with exercises.
Straight snowplow.
Snowplow turns, linked turns.
Side slip in the fall-line.
Forward side slip.
Plow swing, basic swing.
Stem swing, stem short swing.
Basic parallel, parallel, wedeln.

Additional subjects for Grades III, II and I

Skiing at speed in the bumps.
Skiing in difficult snow.

Additional subject for Grades II and I

Setting slalom and giant slalom courses.

Note:

Candidates for Grades II and I must be fully paid-up members of BASI and have taught for one full season (twelve weeks) in a recognized ski school.

Lecture programme

For ski party leader	*For Grade III*
Navigation I	Navigation I
Ski technique I	Ski technique I
Snowcraft and avalanche hazard	Snowcraft and avalanche hazard
Mountain safety and exposure	Mountain safety and exposure
Ski accidents and first aid	Ski accidents and first aid
Ski preparation	Ski preparation
Ski equipment	Ski equipment
Ski party leadership	

184

For Grade II

Revision of navigation I
Revision of ski technique I
Revision of ski accidents and
first aid
Navigation II
Ski technique II
Principles of ski teaching
Mountain weather
Snow survey
Ski stretchers and improvisa-
tion

For Grade I

No lectures, but the following
written examinations must be
sat:
Navigation
Weather
Snowcraft and mountain safety
Ski teaching
Ski equipment
There is also a practical examin-
ation in navigation

Examination programme

	Practical	Pass mark	Written	Pass mark	Additional requirements
Ski party leader	teaching practice	15/20			
	technical ability	15/20			
Grade III	teaching practice	16/20			
	technical ability	16/20			
Grade II	teaching practice	16/20			
	technical ability	16/20			
Grade I	teaching practice	18/20	navigation	50/100	Current BASI
	technical ability	18/20	weather	50/100	licence.
	navigation	50/100	snowcraft and mountain safety	50/100	Full season teaching.
			ski teaching	50/100	Current first
			ski equipment	50/100	aid certificate.

Candidates must obtain a pass in both parts of the skiing examination and, for Grade I, all written examinations, to become qualified. If a person fails one part of the examination by no more than
0.5 below the pass mark, he may apply for re-examination in that
subject alone during any of the next three BASI assessment courses.

Further details of the BASI qualifications and courses are available from the Secretary, BASI, Inch Village Hall, Kincraig,
Inverness-shire.

Appendix H

National qualifications are administered by the Royal Yacht Association (5 Buckingham Gate, London SW1) and by the National Schools Sailing Association, Education Offices, County Hall, Chichester. Local qualifications suited to the particular needs of local education authorities are available. Typical of these is the scheme in Edinburgh outlined below.

EDINBURGH SCHOOLS SAILING ASSOCIATION SAILING CERTIFICATES

Cadet

This qualification aims to ensure that the holder can be carried safely in a dinghy with an experienced helmsman, and has the basic knowledge from which to progress. Sails as a trainee crewman with a qualified helmsman.

Requirements

1. Demonstrate ability to swim 50 m in *unheated* water.
2. The names and functions of the main parts of a dinghy's hull, equipment.
3. How to rig a boat ready for launching.
4. Launching a dinghy from a trolley and getting under way.
5. How to sail a dinghy.
6. Stowing equipment and ensuring safety for the boat ashore *or* at moorings (whichever the candidate will normally be doing).
7. Personal buoyancy—difference between buoyancy aids and life jackets. Ability to put on and secure a life jacket of the type(s) used.
8. The reasons for adequate buoyancy being fitted in a dinghy.
9. What to do in the event of a capsize.
10. Demonstrate ability to tie these knots: reef; half hitches; figure of eight.
11. At least fifteen minutes' sailing in a dinghy with an adult instructor.

Items 3, 4, 5 and 6 will not be subject to a practical test, only to simple question and answer. Items 1, 7, 9 and 11 are considered particularly important, and a candidate who fails to satisfy the tester on even one of these items cannot be passed. Item 1: the tester may agree to accept the assurance of the teacher-in-charge of the school club that the candidate has demonstrated this ability. Candidates who are awarded a Cadet Certificate must start to keep a personal sailing logbook giving for each session: dates; location; conditions; type of boat; purposes; time afloat; incidents; comments. Entries to be brief, but clear and neat.

Crew

This qualification aims to ensure that the holder is competent to crew with an experienced helmsman, can instruct cadets to a limited extent, and has the sound basic knowledge from which to progress to helming. Sails as trainee helmsman—initially with an experienced helmsman.

Requirements

1. Hold a Cadet Certificate.
2. Produce a neat, up-to-date personal logbook. The examiner must be satisfied with the candidate's reliability, experience and seamanship.
3. Understand the interaction of real and apparent winds, and their effects on sails and hull. The use and effect of sails, burgee, rudder, centre board and crew's weight.
4. Know the points of sailing, and the necessary adjustments to the boat when changing from one to another.
5. Check craft's equipment and buoyancy.
6. Demonstrate an ability to rig a dinghy ashore and/or afloat; reefing at that time as necessary.
7. Demonstrate launch from and return to a beach, and/or leave and pick up moorings.
8. Demonstrate competence as crew when sailing briskly round a course.
9. Demonstrate competence as crew during man overboard, and capsize.
10. Demonstrate the ability, in reasonable conditions, to 'helm'

single-handed for man overboard. Ability to avoid capsize or other 'loss' of the boat is important, not polished sailing.

11. Demonstrate an ability to explain the 'why' and 'how' of some of the crew members' duties—simple practical points, no theory.

Items 5, 6, 7, 8, 9 and 10 will normally be demonstrated practically. Items 7, 8, 9 and 10 to be carried out in a dinghy with a competent helmsman. Item 10 will require the helmsman to hand over control. The examiner may accept candidates without Cadet certificates for test as crew, but must then include the cadet requirements in the test.

Helm

This qualification aims to ensure that the holder not only has the basic skills necessary, but is in other respects a suitable, knowledgeable, responsible person to have charge of a sailing dinghy and crew.

Requirements

1. Hold a *Crew* Certificate.
2. Carry out a full capsize drill.
3. Be fully able to take chare of rigging, checking, launching, beaching and mooring of a dinghy.
4. Be able to handle a dinghy safely in wind and sea conditions approaching the club's limits.
5. Have a good understanding of potential dangers and emergency procedures (including recognition and treatment of exposure, and apparent drowning).
6. Be able to use a chart, and plan a day trip with attention to equipment, emergency diversions, landfalls, etc.
7. Be able to evaluate sailing conditions and prospects, and take the correct decisions on launching, reefing, sailing area, crews, etc.
8. Know the basic rules covering 'rights of way' and racing. Have some experience of racing at local club level.
9. Demonstrate the ability to instruct cadet and crew members.
10. Have a good record of reliability and seamanship.

Appendix I

Many colleges of education now offer an introduction to outdoor education as an elective subject. The degree of commitment varies very considerably, but the work is most often undertaken at weekends, not as an integral part of the teaching programme. Notable exceptions to this are at I. M. Marsh College of Physical Education at Liverpool, where a three-year full-time course in Environmental Studies is available, and at Bangor Normal College, where a similar course started in 1972. The only in-service courses resulting in a specific qualification in outdoor education are run in Scotland. Dunfermline College run a one-term course and Moray House College runs a comprehensive full-year course, resulting in the Diploma of Outdoor Education.

MORAY HOUSE COLLEGE OF EDUCATION DIPLOMA COURSE IN OUTDOOR EDUCATION

Duration of course. The course involves full-time attendance at college or at a practical work placement over a period of one academic year.

Approximate Term dates:

Winter Term : 2nd October to 15th December.
Spring Term : 8th January to 23rd March.
Summer Term : 16th April to 14th July.

An expedition takes place during the three weeks immediately following the Summer Term.

Entry qualifications: No precise academic qualifications are prescribed, but preference will be given to qualified teachers and those with teaching experience.

Course costs (in 1973) : The total fee payable to the college on enrolment was £250. This includes tuition fees, £60, and a composite

189

fee, £4. The remainder is intended to meet the placement and other expenses which will be incurred and covers:

(a) expenses when resident in placement outside the college area, including travelling expenses thereto and therefrom (also the expedition expenses to the extent of £50).

(b) fees payable to examining bodies listed in the course outline.

Personal expenditure: The following costs will require to be met by the student:

(a) Subsistence (including lodging) expenses whilst in attendance at college and travelling expenses from home/lodgings to college.

(b) Cost of personal equipment, clothing and books. (A list of these requirements will be provided.)

Secondment: It is anticipated that the large majority of candidates accepted for the course will attend on secondment from their employing authorities. Application for secondment must be made by the applicant.

COURSE OUTLINE

The course programme is divided into the following main areas of study:

Introductory residential week

This short, pre-course get-together has two objectives. Firstly, to allow members of the course to meet each other and the staff in an informal and relaxed atmosphere. Secondly, to permit the staff to make the necessary pre-course assessments of ability and potential in order to be able to direct the students in the best possible way.

The basic course

This will be a common course spread throughout the whole period of training, consisting of those elements which are considered to be essential, irrespective of individual specialisms. Equal emphasis will be given to *countryside studies*, relevant aspects of *education* and *sociology*, and the teaching of *basic outdoor skills*.

190

Outdoor pursuits

Candidates are expected to achieve a responsible standard of proficiency in the major outdoor pursuits listed in column A below. They will be encouraged to proceed towards the high-grade national qualifications, listed in column B.

A

B

The Mountain Leadership Certificate (summer) awarded by the Scottish Mountain Leadership Training Board (SMLTB)

The Mountain Leadership Certificate (winter) awarded by the SMLTB

The Mountain Instructor's Certificate awarded by the SMLTB

Ski Party Leader's Certificate awarded by the Scottish National Ski Council

Grade I, II or III certificates awarded by the British Association of Ski Instructors

National Day Boat Certificate Grade I, awarded by the Royal Yachting Association (RYA)

National Sailing Instructor's Certificate, awarded by the RYA

Certificates awarded by the British Canoe Union (BCU) or the Scottish Canoe Association (SCA)

Certificates awarded by the BCU or SCA

Inland Proficiency (kayak or Canadian)

Inland Advanced (kayak or Canadian) Sea Advanced (kayak)

Sea and Open Water Proficiency (kayak)

Senior Instructor and Coach awards—kayak (sea or inland) or Canadian

Special courses

A limited number of national courses of outstanding value will be included in the programme for all students, e.g.:

(*a*) The Mountaineering Instructor's Certificate training course.
(*b*) The Scottish Mountain Leadership Certificate courses.

(*c*) The British Ski Instruction Council courses.
(*d*) The National Field Study Course.

Teaching practice

Students must have practical teaching experience in three specific areas within the field of outdoor education, in summer and winter conditions.

(*a*) At the National Centre or at a local authority or field study centre.
(*b*) At a school—to organize or assist with a programme of outdoor education.
(*c*) Independently with a school party—camping or at an unstaffed centre or hostel.

As far as possible periods of teaching practice will be continuous. Students with previous experience in one area will devote more time to the unfamiliar situation.

Projects

Two projects will be undertaken during the course of the year. One will be of a practical nature, e.g. canoe building, making a contoured model, photographic work and so on. The other should have some connection with the environment, and should be in a field outside the specialization of the particular student. Topics will be suggested which tend to link activities with a study of a particular aspect of the environment, e.g. rock climbing, with the study of different rock types and structres.

Expeditions

Each course will end with a three-week expedition of an exploratory nature, possibly abroad. The students will participate in its organization but will be accompanied by staff.

Assessment

With the exception of meeting the requirements for national awards, assessment will be of a continuous nature throughout the year. There will be no final examination, although a constructive assessment will be made on projects undertaken by students.

A. *Countryside studies*

The aim of this section of the syllabus is to provide students with the basic knowledge required for an appreciation of the countryside, with particular emphasis on interpretation to young people. Practical work will be undertaken where appropriate, and will be arranged to demonstrate the interrelationships that exist within the whole environment.

1. The ecology of the major habitats in the United Kingdom, i.e. mountain, moorland, woodland, lowland, fresh water and shore.
2. The origins of land forms and in particular the effects on landscape of erosion and deposition. Identification of major rock types, fossils and minerals, and a basic knowledge of their place in the geological pattern. Structural geology and the recognition of major structural features in the field. The study of Scottish gem stones. Basic lapidary techniques.
3. The theoretical study of this subject should be backed up by observations taken on expeditions and at college.
4. A study of the interaction of man and nature in historical times and recognition of how man has modified his environment. The need for conservation and controlled development in the country-side.
5. Major uses of countryside, particularly 'wild' country. An appreciation of the needs and problems of the various users: crofters, farmers, foresters, landowners, fishermen, sportsmen, etc. The multi-purpose use of land and water.
6. The work of national bodies concerned with countryside conservation: The Countryside Commission, Nature Conservancy, National Trust, Forestry Commission and Forest Parks, Scottish Wildlife Trust, RSPB, Council for Nature, Civic Trust. The role of Local Authority, statutory responsibilities and relevant Acts of Parliament. The law relating to access to land and water. Access agreements.
7. Conservation through education: the country code, nature trails, literature and films, information and advisory services, participation by school and youth groups, e.g. Conservation corps, Enterprise Youth and National Trust schemes.
8. Creative Studies: painting, model work, etc.

B. *Education*

9. Special attention will be given to the application and modification of teaching methods in the outdoor situation. Preparation in use of visual aids. Use of photographs, cine and CCTV.
10. Supervised talks from a wide range of subjects. Each student is given two during the year.
11. Physical and psychological development of young people and the relevance of these factors in outdoor activity programming. Programme and training for the primary school child.
12. The acquisition of skills.
13. Group behaviour and relationships.
14. Leadership and leadership techniques.
15. Philosophy, history and organization of outdoor recreation and education.
16. Relevant reports and organizations. Statistical surveying techniques.
17. Physiological considerations. General body metabolism, energy requirements, oxygen consumption, etc. The thermo-regulatory system and responses to hot and cold environments. Hypothermia, exhaustion and exposure.
18. Management studies. Organization and administration of outdoor education schemes, including outdoor centres. Programme planning.
19. Sociology of recreation.
20. Educational psychology.
21. Recreation planning.

C. *Outdoor pursuits*

22. Certain skills may be regarded as common to all outdoor activities, and these should be taught to all students irrespective of their choice of specialist activity:

    Navigation on land and water.
    Orienteering.
    Equipment and clothing design and materials.
    Basic campcraft, including mobile mountain camping.
    Expedition planning, including the organization of expeditions abroad.

First Aid and resuscitation, leading to the basic adult qualification of the St John Ambulance Brigade or the Red Cross Society.

Mountain Safety and the principles of leadership on the hills.

Water safety and the Water Sports Code.

Swimming and life saving.

The Rescue Services, their organization and methods. Basic rescue techniques on the mountain and at sea.

Basic instruction will be given in rock climbing, winter mountaineering, skiing, ski-touring, canoeing, sailing, potholing, skin-diving, etc.

Appendix J

The curriculum caters for both girls and boys from the age of eleven to eighteen.

Ages 11–13

The time available is made up of a two-hour session each week throughout the year, together with weekend camps and culminating in a five day summer camp. These opportunities involve the pupils in inter-disciplinary inquiry projects, and at the same time provide a sound base of map reading and navigational skills.

Ages 13–14

Further opportunities to develop foundation skills, in particular camping experience, are afforded through one-hour meetings each week, weekend expeditions and a five day summer expedition. Mountaineering is introduced into the curriculum through weekend visits to North Wales. In addition to special skills the third-year course eases the problem of integrating pupils who enter the school at thirteen with those who have already been through the first two forms.

Ages 14–15

Established interests are fostered by the specialist school societies and clubs, many of which operate largely independently. Pupils' initiative is encouraged by their own planning of weekend expeditions. Supervised expeditions become progressively more ambitious, and the range of activities is diversified to include sailing, canoeing, rock climbing and pony trekking. Project work, such as the renovation of bothies or preparation of exhibition material, is included throughout the year.

* Abbotsholme School, Rocester, Nr Uttoxeter, Staffordshire.

Academic pressure of sixth-form work means that less time is available for the outdoor education programme, and much of the involvement at this level is undertaken by specialist courses such as the Outward Bound courses. These provide an opportunity to gain another set of values at a time when those established by the school may be subject to question. Selected pupils assist the junior forms in simple hill walking and camping expeditions, experience which is invaluable to those working for the Mountain Leadership certificate.

Expeditions are held during each vacation. These are not necessarily restricted to Britain; indeed some of the summer expeditions are ambitious undertakings to the mountains of Iceland, Norway or the High Atlas. An expedition of this type forms the climax to a school career in outdoor education.

Such a comprehensive and protracted course is largely made possible through the traditions of the school, the enthusiasm of the staff and the local environment. Opportunities to benefit from these provisions are offered to pupils from the public sector of education. Local pupils are invited to join the third-year training programme, and a newly established residential centre near the school is made available to local education authorities, colleges of education and universities.

Abbotsholme provides an excellent example of the opportunities which exist for educational innovations in the private sector, an example which, having been shown to be both feasible and successful, may well be adopted by other progressive authorities.

Index